Cults Utopia 1Q84

Cults Utopia 1Q84

An Enterprise Architecture Review

Eric Tse

CONTENTS

DEDICATION

I dedicate this book to all the children living in cult and non-cult region. Hope this book can bring them joy and the positive energy to live happily.

ACKNOWLEDGMENTS

First of all, I am indebted to my editor, and other reviewers who have suggested several fixes and invaluable feedback for this book. Thanks also to my publisher, Create Space Inc, Xlibris Corporation and Amazon.com for the publication.

Thank you to my family for their ongoing support while I was writing this book.

Thanks are also due to all the healthcare and social work communities, ministries and institutions.

To all of the readers, a sincere thanks for selecting this book and making up your mind to read it. Hopefully you will forget all these after having finished reading the book. (lots of laugh)

1 INTRODUCTION

This literature is NOT real. It is all IMAGINATION. This is an exercise to describe the irrational behaviors of cults using enterprise architecture.

Cult violence is a form of collective behavior characterized by progressive escalation of conflict, internal radicalization, and the impossibility of escape or retreat from the inevitability of extreme violence (Bromley & Melton 2002, O'Connor 2011).

There have been several attempts at modeling cults and sects, but none of them have successfully been able to describe the gist of the beast in a simplistic manner. Moreover, cults have been evolving quickly, utilizing advanced knowledge from different areas. Nonetheless, the underlying principles have not been changed significantly over the years. The author uses a portfolio of models instead, to unify the different views.

The body of knowledge involves a portfolio of multidisciplinary models, theories, processes, methodologies and templates. The main disciplines are business and administration, project/operation management, healthcare, criminology, public administration besides others.

Purpose

This literature is intended to provide a comprehensive yet simplistic idea regarding what cults are regarding, so as to arouse public interest in understanding cults and their irrational behavior.

Cult or *Community* members can identify that some of their activities have a negative impact on the community; which is not correct. Global citizens will be aware of what they do and the impact that it has. Missioners need to be aware of their social responsibilities while performing their duties.

Victims can use this as a self-help support resource to minimize the negative impact that they have been subjected to from existing cults and communities.

Hopefully a better framework and more tools can be established, such that citizens participate by co-operating with the government to manage the social costs generated by the cults and communities.

Scope

We strongly emphasize cults or communities defined in this document are ideology and religion neutral so as to make it widely applicable.

Cults and communities are harassment-centric, and imply the architecture focus on harassment as the main vehicle to expand and sustain enterprise architecture.

The following reasons justify the architecture to be harassment-centric:

— Harassment serve as a main theme that brings out other concepts.
— We try not to reinvent too many wheels.
— We want to differentiate cults from other businesses and operations.
— It is assumed that harassment is the most popular activity in cults.
— Harassment brings severe negative impact to public welfare/healthcare.
— No OPEN, unified, consolidated and systematic body of knowledge has been developed to explain and address this world wide social phenomenon.

Many cults members think terrorism to be illegal, but consider harassment activities as legal and meaningful. They perceive harassment as the most powerful way of helping people, little realizing that their commitments as harmful and illegal.

The scope of literature, extends to topics; such as Concepts of Enterprise Architecture and Cult Models.

However, topics such as correlation between harassment and other criminal activities, and implementation details of cults from models are not touch upon.

Audience

This literature is intended for cults and communities so that they can be made aware of the consequences and impact of what they have been doing. Victims can also get support, recover partially, after going through this book.

If they are made aware about why their lives have been changed and they are sure to recognize that it is not their fault, then they can live life with a more positive perspective.

This book is also likely to make the general audience realize the extent to which harassment-centric cults and communities can impact the world on a daily basis. Hopefully, witnesses can work out strategies in collaboration with their local governments and institutions to control cults and terrorism behavior.

Definitions

1984 is a 1949 dystopian novel by George Orwell about an oligarchical, collectivist society. Life in the Oceanian province of Airstrip One is a world of perpetual war, pervasive government surveillance, and incessant public mind control. The individual is always subordinated to the state, and it is in part this philosophy, which allows the Party to manipulate and control humanity. In the Ministry of Truth, protagonist Winston Smith is a civil servant responsible for perpetuating the Party's propaganda by revising historical records to render the Party omniscient and always correct, yet his meager existence disillusions him to the point of seeking rebellion against Big Brother, eventually leading to his arrest, torture, and re-conversion.—("1984", 2011, "Definition", para. 1)

1Q84 is a novel by Haruki Murakami, first published in three volumes in Japan in 2009-2010. The title is a play on the Japanese pronunciation of the year 1984. The letter Q and the Japanese number 9 are homophones, which are often used in Japanese wordplay. This is a reference to George Orwell's Nineteen Eighty-Four. It tackles themes of murder, history, cult religion, violence, family ties and love. It was also reviewed that the novel "may become a mandatory read for anyone trying to get to grips with contemporary Japanese culture" ("1Q84", 2011, "Definition", para. 1)

Cult is

1. A specific system of religious, ideological beliefs, especially with reference to its rites and deity. The secretive organizations in 1Q84 are best described as cults, or cult community.
2. A quasi-religious organization using devious psychological techniques to gain and control adherents.
3. In this literature, 1Q84 cults are interpreted as an enterprise architecture that operates changes, promotes, maintains, or reinforces such system of beliefs.

Enterprise Architecture (EA) is a rigorous description of the structure of an enterprise, which comprises enterprise components (business entities), the externally visible properties of those components, and the relationships (e.g. the behavior) between them. EA describes the terminology, the composition of enterprise components, and their relationships with the external environment, and the guiding principles for the requirement (analysis), design, and evolution of an enterprise. ("Enterprise Architecture", 2011, "Definition", para. 1). This description is comprehensive, including enterprise goals, business process, roles, organizational structures, organizational behaviors, business information system logic. In this literature I have used Zachman based EA framework to describe the 1Q84 community.

Harassment is a feeling of intense annoyance caused by being tormented, or is the act of tormenting by continued persistent attacks and criticism. ("Harassment", 2011, "Definition", para. 1)

Harassment-centric is the theme, or the focus of this literature towards 1Q84. This implies that harassment is the most common way that cults use to achieve their goals.

Unit is a single thing, a person, or any group of things or persons regarded as an entity.

Identification

In this literature, cults and communities are organizations that bring changes or conversions to a system of beliefs, they can be religious, ideological, philosophical, commercial or institutional.

In this literature, a cult or community is an enterprise architecture that operates changes, promotes, maintains, or reinforces such a system of beliefs.

A mature or developed cult can be or should be a sovereign, that is a supreme, absolute, and uncontrollable power by which an independent state is governed and from which all specific political powers are derived; the intentional independence of a state, combined with the right and power of regulating its internal affairs without foreign interference. ("Soverign", 2011, "Definition", para. 1)

Sovereignty is the power of a state to do everything necessary to govern itself, such as making, executing, and applying laws; imposing and collecting taxes; making war and peace; and forming treaties or engaging in commerce with foreign nations.

A cult is usually a form of sovereign within a sovereign, which is not likely to be sustainable without being situated within a non-cult/traditional sovereign.

A cult normally aggressively expands, through promoting their system of beliefs, engulfing and converting neighbor resources outside the cult's boundary, till it is self-sustainable.

The main difference between cult enterprise architecture and commercial enterprise architecture is that cult enterprise architecture is a super set of commercial enterprise architecture. It involves meta-physical, military and meta-legal components. However, most of the existing components inside a commercial EA can be reused in a cult EA

Cult/community-centric enterprise architecture is a cult architecture leveraging harassment as the main disciplines of maintenance and expansion.

Harassment is an act of systematic and/or continued unwanted and annoying actions of one party or a group, including threats and demands. In our architecture, harassment is the main vehicle to convert targeted units.

Missions, in this literature are projects/ series of systematic events that relate to expansion of cults boundary. This can be in any form, such as public speech, scandal, publications, economic development and education etc. In our harassment-centric architecture, missions are mainly harassment-driven.

Conversion is the process of transforming a unit from initial to target state unit. It is a tangible element, system, component used as an actor in our architecture model. It can be a person, a group of people, a resource, a capital, an institution, or a facility, as long as the boundary and attribute of the unit is clearly defined.

Document Organization

Chapter 1 is an introduction of the book what includes the qualitative background and historical context of cults, such as 1Q84, 1984 and enterprise architecture.

Chapter 2 illustrates the theme Harassment-Centric.

Chapter 3 provides an Enterprise Architecture Overview of the cults using meta-models.

Chapter 4 presents the business models of cult EA.

Chapter 5 talks about enterprise management models of cult EA.

Chapter 6 introduces the models and mechanics of unit harassment EA.

Chapter 7 demonstrates system level harassment EA models.

Chapter 8 presents public level harassment EA models.

Chapter 9 provides a deprogramming section, in a bid to ensure that this literature is not perceived as real.

2 META MODELS

Fig 2-1. Meta Model by knowledge area (Judge 2009)

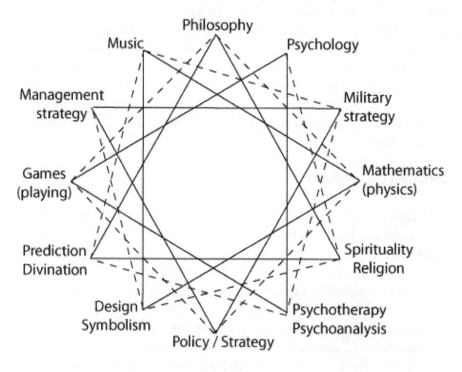

Ref-Code	Name	Description
mm-k-1	Music	NA
mm-k-2	Philosophy	NA
mm-k-3	Psychology	NA
mm-k-4	Military Strategy	NA
mm-k-5	Mathematics (Physics)	NA
mm-k-6	Spirituality Religion	NA
mm-k-7	Psychotherapy/ Psychoanalysis	NA
mm-k-8	Policy / Strategy	NA
mm-k-9	Design Symbolism	NA
mm-k-10	Prediction, Divination	NA
mm-k-11	Games (playing)	NA
mm-k-12	Management Strategy	NA

Fig 2-2. Meta-model by EA (Enterprise Architecture)

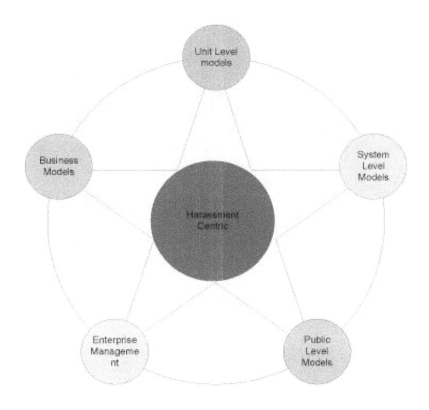

Ref-Code	Name	Description	Disciplines
mm-ea-1	Harassment Centric Concept	Harassment, Stalking. Trespassing, General Harassment Characteristic, Why hard to Investigate?, Motivation.	Criminology, Psychology, Law.
mm-ea-2	Business Architecture Models	Business Visions and Missions, Role Model (s), Use Case model (s), use case by Roles	Business analysis, cults, history, philosophy, Game
mm-ea-3	Enterprise Management Models	Sovereign Models, Enterprise management Model, ERP Models, Roles/Units/ Operations Graphic	History, Philosophy, Geography, Criminology, General Business and Administration, Organization Structure, Enterprise Architecture, Operation Management, Project Management, Game
mm-ea-4	Unit Level Models	Principles, Basic Communication Model, Signal Interpretation Model, Criminal Profiling Model, NLP Model, Why Harassment Centric?, Geographic Profiling,	Cognitive Science, Behavior Science, Human Resource, Psychology, Psychiatry, Psychoanalysis, Psycho-immunology, Criminology, Medical and Health Science, Geography.

mm-ea-5	System Level Models	Causal Model, Spatial Temporary Model, Dynamic Spatial Planning Model, Emotions Wheel Model, Profile Buzzwords Model and Emotion State Transition Model, MLMS Process Model, Spatial-Process Integration Model, Redundancy Model, Event Sequence Model, Harassment Role Model, Scripting Model, Integration and Affiliation Model, Cloud Model, Cult Integration Bus Model, Cult Integration Network Server Model, Multi-disciplinary end points connection Model, Multi-disciplinary integration end points Enumeration (Advanced applied criminology), Community Integration Maturity Model, Harassment Configuration Model, Harassment Configuration Signs and Enumeration Model	Physics, Mathematics, Psychology and Behavior Science, Clinical Psychiatry, Criminology, Cognitive Science, Military, Aerospace, System and Process Engineering, Gaming theory, Information System, Computing Engineering System, System Integration, Advanced applied criminology, Graph Theory and Network, enterprise Organization Management, Chess, Metaphysics, Music and Drama, Enterprise and Application Architecture, Transpiration Theory, Telecommunication Technology, civil engineering, Prediction, Design Symbolism, Software Engineering

mm-ea-6	Public / Social Level Models	Public Administration as Corporate Strategies (Strategy Model), Public Administration Models, Catastrophic events Categorization Model, Lievrouw and Finn's Communication Model, Cult Public Administration Channels Model, Stages Model, Smart Power equalizer Model, Multi-Tier Social Units Model (Government, Public Affairs/Policies, Media, Public), Interpersonal Perspectives Model (McLeod and Steven), The Conflict Model, Caplan's Crisis Model, Social Marketing and Programming Models (Incumbent Models)	Public Administration, Strategic Planning, Disasters Recovery and Business Continuity, Public Safety and National Security, Communication Systems and Cognitive Science, Mass Media, Information Distribution, Military, Sociology, International Affairs, Diplomacy, Conflict Resolution, Marketing, Social ethics, Public Psychology, Risk Management,

There have been several attempts at creating different meta-models to provide a clear summary of all the models. Notice the models I have enumerated are actual enterprise architecture descriptions of the cults.

Similar to the Zachman Enterprise Architecture Framework, these models address the questions (what, how, where, who, when and why), the forms (inventory, process, network, organization, timing, motivation), the structure and components (scope, business concepts, system, logic, technology/physics, component assemblies, operations instances), and, the roles (strategists, owners, designers, builders, implementers, participants). We may not have a 100% clone of the original grid configuration meta-model Zachman Framework, but we have models that address the same concerns, just in a form of Mandela.

The meta-model Medulla divides the topics from the business requirement perspective. The first is the harassment-centric theme that all models are based on as a central concept. All other models revolve around this concept.

Then there are different perspectives of cults; cults as a business unit delivering harassment solutions, cults as an operation to support harassments, unit level harassment activities of cults, system level harassment activities of cults, and social/public administration-level harassment activities of cults.

Within each business category, the models address most enterprise architecture requirements as described in the Zachman Architecture Framework.

3 THEME OF HARASSMENT CENTRIC

What is Harassment?

Harassment covers a wide range of offensive behavior. It is commonly understood as behavior intended to disturb or upset, and it is characteristically repetitive. In the legal sense, it is intentional behavior, which is found threatening or disturbing. ("Harassment", 2011 July 12., "Definition", para. 1)

What is Stalking?

Stalking is a type of secretive, obsessive, and repetitive behavior related to a wider set of behaviors called harassment, intimidation, or threatening. Harassment generally refers to behavior that is psychologically humiliating or abusive. Intimidation generally refers to intentional embarrassment caused by derogatory words or looks. Threatening generally refers to letters or communications intended to strike fear or terror in a victim. Stalking is a more specific type of these general behaviors. (O'Connor, 2010)

What is trespassing

Trespass is an area of tort law broadly divided into three groups: trespass to the person, trespass to chattels and trespass to land.

Trespass to the person, historically involved six separate trespasses: threats, assault, battery, wounding, mayhem, and maiming

Trespass to chattels, also known as trespass to goods or trespass to personal property, is defined as "an intentional interference with the possession of personal property . . . proximately causing injury

Trespass to land, the form of trespass most associated with the term trespass, refers to the "wrongful interference with one's possessory rights in [real] property. ("Trespass", 2011, "Definition", para. 1-4)

General Harassment Characteristic

While stalking almost always involves following a person, the behavior can take place in a variety of locations and in a variety of ways—at or near a person's home or place of business, making harassing phone calls, leaving written messages or objects, or vandalizing a person's property

Any communication between stalker and victim is nonconsensual communication. There is usually some danger or threat made explicit or implicit that harm will come to the victim

Harassment-centric

It is the theme, the whole point or the focus of cults. This implies harassment is the most common way cults use to achieve their goals. Cults are set up because they want to harass. The business objectives of cults are to support harassment. Cults maintain their operations like a Kingdom or Sovereign because they want to harass better. The unit models are what, why, when, who, how cults harass as units. The system models are what, why, when, who, how cults harass as systems. The public models are what, why, when, who how cults harass as communities, social movements and social marketing engines.

Why hard to investigate?

As a behavior, stalking presents significant problems to investigation owing to the variety of behaviors present, the fact that the origins and dynamics of the crime are poorly understood, and because the crime is as likely to comprise mental as well as physical elements. (Turvey, 1999)

What motivates cults to harass?

There are different classes of motivations. The following criminology models may best describe the motivations between individuals. (O'Connor, 2010)

(Gerberth, 2006: 751-57) and (O'Connor, 2010)

Ref-Code	Psychopathic Personality Stalker	Psychotic Personality Stalker
mv-gerberth-01-mmea1	Invariably male	Can be male or female
mv-gerberth-02-mmea1	Largest population of stalkers	Becomes obsessed and/or preoccupied with systematized delusions
mv-gerberth-03-mmea1	Comes from abusive home and dysfunctional family	Diagnosed mental disorder may include paranoia, schizophrenia, bipolar or affective disorder-manic-depressive
mv-gerberth-04-mmea1	Violence was the normal way to settle family disputes	The target is a delusional fixation
mv-gerberth-05-mmea1	Offender and his mother were domestic abuse victims	Target is usually a stranger
mv-gerberth-06-mmea1	Is a control freak	Can target coworkers, neighbors, acquaintances
mv-gerberth-07-mmea1	Is easily frustrated	Attempt to contact target to let them know of their existence
mv-gerberth-08-mmea1	Cannot take responsibility for his actions	Activities include telephone calls, letters, gifts, visits, surveillance

mv-gerberth-09-mmea1	Offender insists on male dominance	A subtype is erotomania which involves belief that the target is in love with them, or they are in love with the target
mv-gerberth-10-mmea1	Shows a hyper-macho exterior	NA
mv-gerberth-11-mmea1	Harbors hostility toward women and has abusive relationships	NA
mv-gerberth-12-mmea1	If a woman attempts to end the relationship, he will respond with violence	NA
mv-gerberth-13-mmea1	Crime behaviors include vandalizing property, sending packages or deliveries, poison or kill pets, anonymous telephone calls, anonymous threats, other forms of harassment	NA

(Bennett and Hess, 2007) and (Wood and Wood, 2002) and (O'Connor, 2010)

Ref-Code	types	Description
mv-bhww-01-mmea1	Erotomania:	This category was 9.5 % of the cases studied. The Stalker falsely believes that the target, usually someone famous or rich, is in love with the stalker. The victim does not know the stalker. This group usually consists of women targeting males, and is the least dangerous of the three groups.

mv-bhww-02-mmea1	Love **Obsession:**	This category consisted of 43% of the cases studied. The stalker is a stranger to the target but is obsessed and mounts a campaign of harassment to make the target aware of their existence. Ninety-seven percent of these stalkers were male, between the ages of 30 and 40 years of age, and their victims were aged between 20 to 30. The stalkers learned of their victim through the media and did not know them in actuality. Twenty-five percent of these stalkers made threats to their targets, but only 3 % carried them out.
mv-bhww-03-mmea1	Simple Obsession:	This category made up 47 % of the cases studied. The stalker is usually a male (80%), knows the target as an ex-spouse, ex-lover, or former boss, and begins a campaign of harassment. This group is socially immature, unable to develop lasting relationships, shows extreme jealousy, insecurity, paranoia, and feelings of helplessness and powerlessness.

However, from the cults or communities perspective, organized or not organized harassment/stalking/ trespassing events or programs, social movements, are considered as religious missions, which is a mandatory commitment for members.

The end goals of such events are supposed to be aligned with visions and missions to the cultic kingdom as a whole. These include attempts to manipulate target objects, spiritual and organization ego, funding, marketing and sales, more members, sovereign expansion, more wealth, political agendas, new members conversion, public administration, spiritual-artistic performances, demonstration of power, sense of executing punishment, sense of achievement as a whole, commercial and professional demonstration, feeling attack rivalry or in defense of the sovereign.

Nowadays, for cults and communities, harassment/stalking-centric mission framework becomes *de facto* and the most common 'military practices' of cults and communities.

4 BUSINESS MODELS

Ref-Code	Name	Description
	Visions and Missions Model	Enumeration of visions and missions of running the cults as a strategists, King or CEO
	Role Models	There are different ways to categorize different functionalities of the population inside cults. It can be roles as social class, or role as different color (*ad-hoc*, political inference).
	Use Case Models	Enumeration different uses of different roles inside the cults
	Use Cases by King	NA
	Use Cases by Nobles	NA
	Use Cases by Knights	NA
	Use Cases by Members	NA
	Use Cases to Non members, Ex members	NA
	Use Case by Sponsors, Affiliates	NA

Mission and Vision Models

Assume you are the king or CEO of the cults or the organization, what are the ultimate goals, higher level mission and visions you would like to achieve?

Ref-Code	Missions and visions
mv-1-mmea2	The cults and communities are effectively sovereigns and sub-sovereigns.
mv-2-mmea2	I am the King of the sovereigns. Members need obedience.
mv-3-mmea2	Conquer all provinces (counties) / Conquer 10 provinces (counties).
mv-4-mmea2	Maximize cults' member faith.
mv-5-mmea2	100% population in my sovereigns practices my faith.
mv-6-mmea2	People who do not practice our common values and faith have to suffer.
mv-7-mmea2	Lots of wealth, land, ego and power.
mv-8-mmea2	Our members and influence are everywhere.
mv-9-mmea2	Our generals and our heroes are useful and competitive.
mv-10-mmea2	We control everything, including every social units, every instant of my people's lives.
mv-11-mmea2	Lots of fear if not obey, some joy if obey.
mv-12-mmea2	We know everything about everyone's life. We control your destiny.
mv-13-mmea2	Lots of propaganda, social movement, died and conquer our enemies or areas that do not belongs to us.
mv-14-mmea2	I want my off-springs to heir the kingdom.

Role Model (Social Class)

This is a set of roles normally recognized in the business architectures. In simpler terms these set of roles represents the social class of the enterprise architecture.

Notice there are other sets of roles, used from a different perspective, such as different roles of soldiers under active mission events.

Ref-Code	Name	Description
r-sc-1-mmea2	King	Owner of the cults and communities, B2E
r-sc-2-mmea2	Nobles	Special Class that have executives rights, responsibilities, ownership and access, B2E

r-sc-3-mmea2	Knights	Management role that manipulate members and control events, B2E
r-sc-4-mmea2	Members	Mass contributors, B2E
r-sc-5-mmea2	Non members	Targeted members and enemies, B2E
r-sc-6-mmea2	Ex members	Targeted enemies
r-sc-7-mmea2	Sponsors	External B2B, B2C, input money, get service
r-sc-8-mmea2	Affiliates	External B2B, balance power

Role Model (Different Colors, Virtual Class, *ad-hoc*)

This model differentiates actors using different colors. There are no solid pre-defined meaning of each color. However these set of colored actors are usually used in different harassment processes and events, such as the ones in subsequent sectors. There can be inference meanings. Implementers can defined color's meanings in different occasions.

Ref-Code	Name	Description
r-dc-1-mmea2	Red	
r-dc-2-mmea2	Blue	
r-dc-3-mmea2	Black	
r-dc-4-mmea2	Purple	
r-dc-5-mmea2	Green	
r-dc-6-mmea2	Brown	

Use Case Model

Use case modeling is description of business or system functionalities between different actors (different roles) and the systems (cults).

Use Cases by King

Think yourself like a King.
As a King, what features would you like to have?

Ref-Code	Name	Description
u-sc-1-mmea2	Get more money	NA
u-sc-2-mmea2	Get more people	NA
u-sc-3-mmea2	Get more power	NA
u-sc-4-mmea2	Get more property	NA
u-sc-5-mmea2	Get more penetration	NA
u-sc-6-mmea2	Get more control	NA
u-sc-7-mmea2	Get more obedience	NA
u-sc-8-mmea2	All people can get manipulated easily and contribute	NA
u-sc-9-mmea2	Get more sponsorships	NA
u-sc-10-mmea2	Milk our People	NA
u-sc-11-mmea2	Kill our Enemy	NA
u-sc-12-mmea2	Join us good, leave us bad	NA
u-sc-13-mmea2	Lots of Fear	NA
u-sc-14-mmea2	Expand our territory	NA
u-sc-15-mmea2	People get penalized and suffered if not obey	NA
u-sc-16-mmea2	As much wives and kids as you want	NA

Use Case by Sponsors, Affiliates

As Sponsors, what features would you like them to have?

Ref-Code	Name	Description
u-sc-17-mmea2	Sponsorship	Sponsor funding (Large Sum)
u-sc-18-mmea2	Act on Organization	Sponsors want community to handle an organization that the sponsors cannot handle with
u-sc-19-mmea2	Act on Community	Sponsors want community to handle another community that the sponsors cannot handle with
u-sc-20-mmea2	Act on Groups	Sponsors want community to handle another Group that the sponsors cannot handle with
u-sc-21-mmea2	Act on People	Sponsors want community to handle another People that the sponsors cannot handle with
u-sc-22-mmea2	Recruit People	Sponsors want community to handle another Group that the sponsors cannot handle with
u-sc-23-mmea2	Act on Events	Sponsors want community to organize events
u-sc-24-mmea2	Advertisement	Sponsors want community to advertise
u-sc-25-mmea2	Social Support	Sponsors want community to interface with and get support from social units that sponsors do not have
u-sc-26-mmea2	Situated Environmental Support	Sponsors want the environment that the sponsors organization situated in get enough support, so that everything can run smoothly.
u-sc-27-mmea2	Purchase Noble positions	Sponsors want to be noble for some reasons, so that they can utilize the community to a larger extent.

Use Cases by Nobles

As Nobles, what features would you like them to have?

Ref-Code	Name	Description
u-sc-28-mmea2	Obey the King	NA
u-sc-29-mmea2	Work hard for the King	NA
u-sc-30-mmea2	Control members and knights	NA
u-sc-31-mmea2	Milk more from the People	NA
u-sc-32-mmea2	Declare more expansion events	NA
u-sc-33-mmea2	Maximize social impact	NA
u-sc-34-mmea2	Manage operations	NA
u-sc-35-mmea2	Design and Implement and manage harassment initiatives	NA
u-sc-36-mmea2	Spread, Spread, Spread	NA
u-sc-37-mmea2	Penetration and Propaganda	NA
u-sc-38-mmea2	Think new ways to match King's goals	NA
u-sc-39-mmea2	Leverage existing effective ways to match King's goals	NA
u-sc-40-mmea2	Get punished if one does not meet requirement	NA
u-sc-41-mmea2	Increase operation and harassment effectiveness	NA
u-sc-42-mmea2	Publications, social Media, and public administrations	NA
u-sc-43-mmea2	Evade problems for the community	NA
u-sc-44-mmea2	Co-ordinate with other Nobles	NA
u-sc-45-mmea2	Diplomatic Events	NA
u-sc-46-mmea2	High level monitoring	NA
u-sc-47-mmea2	Higher level missions/campaigns/ movements	NA
u-sc-48-mmea2	Knights procurement and management	NA
u-sc-49-mmea2	Acts as ministers for different ministries	NA

Use Cases by Knights

As Knights, what features would you like them to have?

Ref-Code	Name	Description
u-sc-50-mmea2	Obey the King and nobles	NA
u-sc-51-mmea2	Work hard for the King and nobles	NA
u-sc-52-mmea2	Milk more from the People	NA
u-sc-53-mmea2	Execute expansion events	NA
u-sc-54-mmea2	Manipulate and train members during group events	NA
u-sc-55-mmea2	Design, Implement and manage harassment initiatives (Execution Level)	NA
u-sc-56-mmea2	Get punished if one does not meet requirement	NA
u-sc-57-mmea2	Increase operation and harassment effectiveness by manipulating members	NA
u-sc-58-mmea2	Punish members if they do not obey	NA
u-sc-59-mmea2	Lead and Support members during harassment events	NA
u-sc-60-mmea2	Execute tasks for operation management	NA
u-sc-61-mmea2	Spy and information collection and profiling	NA
u-sc-62-mmea2	Lead members recruitment activities	NA
u-sc-63-mmea2	Responsible for conversion performance	NA
u-sc-64-mmea2	Monitoring members and report activities	NA
u-sc-65-mmea2	Track members, non-members, and ex members	NA
u-sc-66-mmea2	Attack non-members or ex members	NA
u-sc-67-mmea2	For larger harassment movements, obey and execute upon directions from kings or nobles	NA
u-sc-68-mmea2	Establish lower level groups in penetration areas	NA
u-sc-69-mmea2	Execute retention policy	NA
u-sc-70-mmea2	Motivate members for all harassment centric activities	NA
u-sc-71-mmea2	Multidisciplinary with different specialties and career Paths	NA
u-sc-72-mmea2	Can have one beautiful spouse	NA
u-sc-73-mmea2	Select spouse for non-members	NA

Use Cases by Members

As members, what features would you like them to have?

Ref-Code	Name	Description
u-sc-74-mmea2	Contribute time	NA
u-sc-75-mmea2	Contribute wealth	NA
u-sc-76-mmea2	Contribute talent for expansion	NA
u-sc-77-mmea2	Contribute to operation tasks	NA
u-sc-78-mmea2	Contribute Life	NA
u-sc-79-mmea2	Contribute by producing kids	NA
u-sc-80-mmea2	Contribute by getting new members in	NA
u-sc-81-mmea2	Contribute by not letting members go away	NA
u-sc-82-mmea2	Contribute by profiling new members	NA
u-sc-83-mmea2	Engaged in participating harassment processes and events	NA
u-sc-84-mmea2	Contribute by harassing targets	
u-sc-85-mmea2	Members feel superior, non-members feel inferior	NA
u-sc-86-mmea2	Members have jobs, non-members no jobs	NA
u-sc-87-mmea2	Members have families, non-members have no families	NA
u-sc-88-mmea2	Members can criticize and harass non-members, but not vice versa	NA
u-sc-89-mmea2	Members is adult, non-members as kids	NA
u-sc-90-mmea2	Members can have kids, non-members cannot have kids	NA
u-sc-91-mmea2	Members can give feedback to non-members, but not vice versa	NA
u-sc-92-mmea2	Members can have good health, non-members cannot	NA
u-sc-93-mmea2	Members should isolate new members from their original friends, and families, unless they are willing to get them in the community	NA
u-sc-94-mmea2	Members can own vehicle, non-members cannot	NA
u-sc-95-mmea2	Members can perform better, non-members cannot	NA

u-sc-96-mmea2	Members can have propensity, non members cannot	NA
u-sc-97-mmea2	Members can feel blessed and have good luck, non members cannot	NA
u-sc-98-mmea2	Members get more information, non members cannot	NA
u-sc-99-mmea2	Members get support, non-members get attacked	NA
u-sc-100-mmea2	Harass by insulting	NA
u-sc-101-mmea2	Harass by accusing	NA
u-sc-102-mmea2	Harass by sexual abusing	NA
u-sc-103-mmea2	Harass by abusing	NA
u-sc-104-mmea2	Harass by manipulating	NA
u-sc-105-mmea2	Harass by providing feedback	NA
u-sc-106-mmea2	Harass by stalking	NA
u-sc-107-mmea2	Harass by domestic abusing	NA
u-sc-108-mmea2	Harass by profiling	NA
u-sc-109-mmea2	Harass by feeding information	NA
u-sc-110-mmea2	Harass by cyber crime	NA
u-sc-111-mmea2	Harass by workplace discrimination	NA
u-sc-112-mmea2	Harass by hate events	NA
u-sc-113-mmea2	Harass by Mass Media	NA
u-sc-114-mmea2	Harass by bullying	NA
u-sc-115-mmea2	Harass by deprivation	NA
u-sc-116-mmea2	Harass by divide and conquer	NA
u-sc-117-mmea2	Harass by deceiving	NA
u-sc-118-mmea2	Harass by emotion manipulation	NA
u-sc-119-mmea2	Harass by artificial testimony	NA
u-sc-120-mmea2	Harass by misleading	NA
u-sc-121-mmea2	Harass by seducing	NA
u-sc-122-mmea2	Harass by publishing	NA
u-sc-123-mmea2	Harass by cyber attack	NA
u-sc-124-mmea2	Harass by moral attack	NA
u-sc-125-mmea2	Freezing counter-attack by pleasing	NA

Use Cases to Non members, Ex members, Enemies

As harassment centric events, what would you like your targets to have from the events?

Ref-Code	Name	Description
u-sc-126-mmea2	Harass to be unhappy	NA
u-sc-127-mmea2	Harass to be depressed	NA
u-sc-128-mmea2	Harass to be crazy	NA
u-sc-129-mmea2	Harass to generate illusion	NA
u-sc-130-mmea2	Harass to be disabled	NA
u-sc-131-mmea2	Harass to be mad	NA
u-sc-132-mmea2	Harass to be angry	NA
u-sc-133-mmea2	Harass to be over happy	NA
u-sc-134-mmea2	Harass to lose money	NA
u-sc-135-mmea2	Harass to be sick	NA
u-sc-136-mmea2	Harass to die	NA
u-sc-137-mmea2	Harass to lose job	NA
u-sc-138-mmea2	Harass to lose occupation	NA
u-sc-139-mmea2	Harass to be dying	NA
u-sc-140-mmea2	Harass to explode	NA
u-sc-141-mmea2	Harass to get into scandal	NA
u-sc-142-mmea2	Harass to be infamous	NA
u-sc-143-mmea2	Harass to lose luck	NA
u-sc-144-mmea2	Harass to be frozen	NA
u-sc-145-mmea2	Harass to be catastrophic	NA
u-sc-146-mmea2	Harass to generate disasters	NA
u-sc-147-mmea2	Harass to lose career	NA
u-sc-148-mmea2	Harass to lose family	NA
u-sc-149-mmea2	Harass to lose support	NA
u-sc-150-mmea2	Harass to faith	NA
u-sc-151-mmea2	Harass to be shocked	NA
u-sc-152-mmea2	Harass to lose organizations	NA
u-sc-153-mmea2	Harass to lose sovereigns	NA
u-sc-154-mmea2	Harass to lose groups	NA
u-sc-155-mmea2	Harass to lose charm and confidence	NA

u-sc-156-mmea2	Harass to lose spouse	NA
u-sc-157-mmea2	Harass to change orientation	NA
u-sc-158-mmea2	Harass to fall down	NA
u-sc-159-mmea2	Harass to degrade	NA
u-sc-160-mmea2	Harass to lust	NA
u-sc-161-mmea2	Harass to steal	NA
u-sc-162-mmea2	Harass to kill	NA
u-sc-163-mmea2	Harass to be raped	NA
u-sc-164-mmea2	Harass to get vandalized	NA
u-sc-165-mmea2	Harass to get corrupted	NA
u-sc-166-mmea2	Harass to get propagated	NA
u-sc-167-mmea2	Harass to lose healing capabilities	NA
u-sc-168-mmea2	Harass to lose kids or babies	NA
u-sc-169-mmea2	Using animal to harass	NA
u-sc-170-mmea2	Harass to eat, or not to eat	NA
u-sc-171-mmea2	Harass to feel pain	NA
u-sc-172-mmea2	Harass to be embarrassed	NA
u-sc-173-mmea2	Harass to be rumored	NA
u-sc-174-mmea2	Harass to be defamed	NA
u-sc-175-mmea2	Harass to be stalked	NA
u-sc-176-mmea2	Harass to get mal-functioned	NA
u-sc-177-mmea2	Harass to convert	NA
u-sc-178-mmea2	Harass to get car-crashed	NA
u-sc-179-mmea2	Harass to get into trauma	NA
u-sc-180-mmea2	Harass to get into wars	NA
u-sc-181-mmea2	Harass to get jealous	NA
u-sc-182-mmea2	Harass to get sued	NA
u-sc-183-mmea2	Harass to et confuse	NA
u-sc-184-mmea2	Harass to get poor	NA
u-sc-185-mmea2	Harass to get injured	NA
u-sc-186-mmea2	Harass to get into jail	NA
u-sc-187-mmea2	Harass to get out of business	NA
u-sc-188-mmea2	Harass to control and manipulate	NA
u-sc-189-mmea2	Harass to get bankrupt	NA
u-sc-190-mmea2	Harass to control weather and disaster	NA

u-sc-191-mmea2	Harass to change policy	NA
u-sc-192-mmea2	Harass to get luck	NA
u-sc-193-mmea2	Harass to get or loss prosperity	NA
u-sc-194-mmea2	Harass to age	NA
u-sc-195-mmea2	Harass to get a raise	NA
u-sc-196-mmea2	Harass to get into disasters	NA
u-sc-197-mmea2	Harass to get into terrorism	NA
u-sc-198-mmea2	Harass to penetrate	NA
u-sc-199-mmea2	Harass to promote	NA
u-sc-200-mmea2	Harass to market	NA
u-sc-201-mmea2	Harass to get or lose contract	NA
u-sc-202-mmea2	Harass to change lives	NA
u-sc-203-mmea2	Harass to lose in gamble	NA
u-sc-204-mmea2	Harass to be hospitalized	NA
u-sc-205-mmea2	Harass to get burned	NA
u-sc-206-mmea2	Harass to get daemons	NA
u-sc-207-mmea2	Harass to get constipation	NA
u-sc-208-mmea2	Harass to get stroke	NA
u-sc-209-mmea2	Harass to get heart attack	NA
u-sc-210-mmea2	Harass to commit suicide	NA
u-sc-211-mmea2	Harass to fight against each other	NA
u-sc-212-mmea2	Harass to integrate	NA
u-sc-213-mmea2	Harass to disintegrate	NA
u-sc-214-mmea2	Harass to get threatened	NA
u-sc-215-mmea2	Harass to get in secured	NA
u-sc-216-mmea2	Harass to make wrong decision	NA
u-sc-217-mmea2	Harass to lie	NA
u-sc-218-mmea2	Harass to deprive sleep	NA
u-sc-219-mmea2	Harass to deprive sense	NA
u-sc-220-mmea2	Harass to feel inferior	NA
u-sc-221-mmea2	Harass to lose senses	NA
u-sc-222-mmea2	Harass to tangle	NA
u-sc-223-mmea2	Harass to spin	NA
u-sc-224-mmea2	Harass to get diabetes	NA
u-sc-225-mmea2	Harass to get obese	NA

u-sc-226-mmea2	Harass to get cold	NA
u-sc-227-mmea2	Harass to discriminate	NA
u-sc-228-mmea2	Harass to get discriminated	NA
u-sc-229-mmea2	Harass to lose dignity	NA
u-sc-230-mmea2	Harass to accuse of something not done	NA
u-sc-231-mmea2	Harass to deny	NA
u-sc-232-mmea2	Harass to be optimized or de-optimized	NA

5 ENTERPRISE MANAGEMENT MODEL

Ref-Code	Name	Description
	Sovereign Model	As a Kingdom or Empire, what are the basic components we should have?
	Enterprise Operation Management Model	As a company or association, what are the basic components we should have?
	ERP Models	Enterprise resource planning (ERP) integrates internal and external management information across an entire organization, embracing finance/accounting, HR, manufacturing, sales and service, CRM, etc.
	Roles, Units, Operations Graphic	An individual, group, structure, or other entity regarded as an elementary structural or functional constituent of a whole.

Think yourself as a King. How are you going to view your Kingdom from a bird's eye business perspective?

What are basic processes and concepts you have so as to keep the Kingdom running and expanding?

Although these set of models are not harassment centric, they are vital to the cults enterprise architecture.

Sovereign Models

Sovereignty is the quality of having supreme, independent authority over a geographic area, such as a territory. It can be found in a power to rule and make laws that rest on a political fact for which no purely legal explanation can be provided.

In a cult or community, kings and nobles have absolute power. As a member, you can only obey and contribute. Keeping this mentality in mind is vital.

Sovereign as a massive body wielding a *sword* and Crosier and composed of many individual people (The frontispiece of Hobbes' Leviathan)

Ref-Code	Name	Description
sov-1-mmea3	Civil Services	Nobles: Talk care of all Kingdom Services
sov-2-mmea3	Territories and other Properties	Lands, boarders, castles, cannons, chariots, weapons
sov-3-mmea3	Law	Set of Rules to Obey
sov-4-mmea3	Punishment	
sov-5-mmea3	Military	Expansion and defense, training troops, Tax and Corps collection
sov-6-mmea3	Money, Finance & Corps	
sov-7-mmea3	Communication	Information distribution, control, troops transportation.
sov-8-mmea3	Social Class and People Control	Monitor people productivity and Loyalty, Tax collection
sov-9-mmea3	Diplomacy	Intra-sovereign matters and issues
sov-10-mmea3	Secretary and Literacy	Writing, publishing, education

| sov-11-mmea3 | Apprenticeship and alchemy | Build weapons, units, invent or engineer harassment frameworks etc |
| sov-12-mmea3 | Trade | Within a sovereign barter, import/export |

Operations Management Models

Ref-Code	Name	Description
opm-1-mmea3	Competitiveness, Strategy, and Productivity	NA
opm-2-mmea3	Forecasting	NA
opm-3-mmea3	Product/Service, Work System, Process and Layout Design	NA
opm-4-mmea3	Capacity planning	NA
opm-5-mmea3	Supply Chain Management	NA
opm-6-mmea3	MRP, ERP, MPS, and JIT	NA
opm-7-mmea3	Inventory Management and Scheduling	NA
opm-8-mmea3	Quality Management and Quality Control	NA
opm-9-mmea3	Project Management	NA
opm-10-mmea3	Waiting Lines and Simulation	NA
opm-11-mmea3	Competitiveness, Strategy, and Productivity	NA
opm-12-mmea3	Forecasting	NA

Enterprise Resource Planning model

Ref-Code	Name	Description
erp-1-mmea3	Pushes orders into production vs. pulling as a result of Customer demand	MRP
erp-2-mmea3	Computerized tool to handle numerous yet simple calculations to determine material and timing needs	MRP
erp-3-mmea3	Runs (or regents) periodically, usually weekly	MRP
erp-4-mmea3	Closed Loop mrp allows for feedback from production to facilitate schedule changes.	MRP
erp-5-mmea3	Schedule Capacity, Shipments, Tool Changes & Design Work	MRPII
erp-6-mmea3	Track and Plan the Financial Implications of the Manufacturing Process	MRPIII

erp-7-mmea3	Project Labor Shortages/Excess	MRPIV
erp-8-mmea3	Generate a Single Schedule Acted on by all Functions	MRPV
erp-9-mmea3	Look beyond the Manufacturing's organizational borders	ERP
erp-10-mmea3	Use data shared throughout the Enterprise	ERP
erp-11-mmea3	Apply the same Best Practices across the Enterprise	ERP
erp-12-mmea3	Utilizes State-of-the-Art Technology	ERP

Roles, Units, Operations Graphic

An individual, group, structure, or other entity regarded as an elementary structural or functional constituent of a whole.

Units are grouped into many tables for different business purposes. The following are some of the fundamental units:

Identity Units

Ref-Code	Name	Description
u-id-1-mmea3	User	NA
u-id-2-mmea3	Group	NA
u-id-3-mmea3	Organization	NA
u-id-4-mmea3	Property	Printers, Castles, Microwave etc

Group

Ref-Code	Name	Description
u-grp-1-mmea3	Network	NA
u-grp-2-mmea3	Cell Group	NA
u-grp-3-mmea3	Alumni	NA
u-grp-4-mmea3	Functional Group	NA
u-grp-5-mmea3	Interests Group	NA
u-grp-6-mmea3	Company	NA
u-grp-7-mmea3	School	NA
u-grp-8-mmea3	Class	NA
u-grp-9-mmea3	Chapter	NA

Organization

Ref-Code	Name	Description
u-org-1-mmea3	United Nations	NA
u-org-2-mmea3	IMF	NA
u-org-3-mmea3	CIA	NA

Concept of Operation Graphic (CONOGS)

A verbal or graphic statement, in broad outline, of a commander's assumptions or intent in regard to an operation or series of operations. The concept of operations frequently is embodied in campaign plans and operation plans; in the latter case, particularly when the plans cover a series of connected operations to be carried out simultaneously or in succession. The concept is designed to give an overall picture of the operation. It is included primarily for additional clarity of purpose.

Ref-Code	Name		Description
u-og-1-mmea3	Multiple Sovereigns, Regions, (Affiliates View)		NA
u-og-2-mmea3	Region (operation View)		NA
u-og-3-mmea3	Region (Bird's Eye View)		NA
u-og-4-mmea3	Region (war View)		NA

u-og-5-mmea3	Region (Properties View)		NA
u-og-6-mmea3	Region (Macro War Board View)		NA
u-og-7-mmea3	Street Level (Micro War Board View)		NA
u-og-8-mmea3	Street Level (War view)		NA

Fig 5-1. Various PC CONOGS Game Screen Shots (TECMO KOEI CO. LTD., 2005) and (SQUARE ENIX, 2008)

Role Model-Military Rank

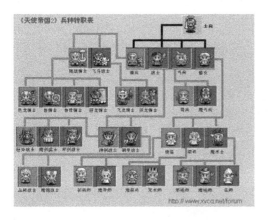

Fig 5-2. Military Rank Game Screen Shots (UserJoy Technology, 2006).

Ref-Code	Name	Description
r-milrnk-1-mmea3	Soldiers	NA
r-milrnk-2-mmea3	Knights	NA
r-milrnk-3-mmea3	Warrior	NA
r-milrnk-4-mmea3	Archer	NA
r-milrnk-5-mmea3	Nun	NA
r-milrnk-6-mmea3	Land Knights	NA
r-milrnk-7-mmea3	Pegasus warrior	NA
r-milrnk-8-mmea3	Sword warrior	NA
r-milrnk-9-mmea3	Armor warrior	NA
r-milrnk-10-mmea3	Crossbow archer	NA
r-milrnk-11-mmea3	Spiritual archer	NA
r-milrnk-12-mmea3	Monk	NA
r-milrnk-13-mmea3	Priest	NA
r-milrnk-14-mmea3	Magician	NA
r-milrnk-15-mmea3	Axe warrior	NA
r-milrnk-16-mmea3	Daemon sword warrior	NA
r-milrnk-17-mmea3	Wicked sword warrior	NA
r-milrnk-18-mmea3	Dual Mode warrior	NA
r-milrnk-19-mmea3	Daemon Spear warrior	NA
r-milrnk-20-mmea3	Express Dragon Knight	NA
r-milrnk-21-mmea3	Lion Knight	NA
r-milrnk-22-mmea3	Lion Face Knight	NA
r-milrnk-23-mmea3	Jumbo Dragon Knight	NA
r-milrnk-24-mmea3	Flying Dragon Knight	NA
r-milrnk-25-mmea3	Spirit Dragon Knight	NA
r-milrnk-26-mmea3	Prayer Master	NA
r-milrnk-27-mmea3	Spiritual Training Master	NA
r-milrnk-28-mmea3	Spiritual Priest	NA
r-milrnk-29-mmea3	Curse Master	NA
r-milrnk-30-mmea3	Wicked magic master	NA
r-milrnk-31-mmea3	Spiritual magic master	NA
r-milrnk-32-mmea3	Wizard	NA

Role Model: Hacking/Terrorist Networks (O'Connor, 2011 Mar 09).

Ref-Code	Name	Description
r-terr-1-mmea3	Organizers	Core members who steer group
r-terr-2-mmea3	Insulators	Members who protect the core
r-terr-3-mmea3	Communicators	Pass on directives
r-terr-4-mmea3	Guardians	Security enforcers
r-terr-5-mmea3	Extenders	Recruiters of new members
r-terr-6-mmea3	Monitors	Advisors about group weaknesses
r-terr-7-mmea3	Members	Those who do the hacking
r-terr-8-mmea3	Crossovers	People with regular jobs
r-terr-9-mmea3	Leadership	Charismatic who lead group
r-terr-10-mmea3	Bodyguards	Members who protect leaders
r-terr-11-mmea3	Seconds in command	Pass on orders
r-terr-12-mmea3	Intelligence	And counterintelligence agents
r-terr-13-mmea3	Financiers	Fund raisers & money launderers
r-terr-14-mmea3	Logistics	Keepers of safe houses
r-terr-15-mmea3	Operations	Those who commit the terror
r-terr-16-mmea3	Sleepers	Members living under deep cover

Cults Operation Units

Ref-Code	Name	Description
u-op-1-mmea3	Governor House	NA
u-op-2-mmea3	Weapon smith	NA
u-op-3-mmea3	City wall	NA
u-op-4-mmea3	Scout camp	NA
u-op-5-mmea3	Bunker	NA
u-op-6-mmea3	Armor smith	NA
u-op-7-mmea3	Drill ground	NA
u-op-8-mmea3	Stable	NA
u-op-9-mmea3	Manson	NA
u-op-10-mmea3	Barracks	NA
u-op-11-mmea3	Ironworks	NA
u-op-12-mmea3	Library	NA

u-op-13-mmea3	Career center	NA
u-op-14-mmea3	Builders guild	NA
u-op-15-mmea3	Warehouse	NA
u-op-16-mmea3	Market	NA
u-op-17-mmea3	Hidden warehouse	NA
u-op-18-mmea3	Granary	NA
u-op-19-mmea3	Command center	NA
u-op-20-mmea3	Tower	NA
u-op-21-mmea3	Cults newspaper center	NA
u-op-22-mmea3	Cults TV	NA
u-op-23-mmea3	Cults Radio	NA
u-op-24-mmea3	Cults Arm and weapon center	NA
u-op-25-mmea3	Cults Financial professional organization network	NA
u-op-26-mmea3	Cults writers and publishers network	NA
u-op-27-mmea3	Cults radiology network	NA
u-op-28-mmea3	Cults drug house	NA
u-op-29-mmea3	Cults day care center	NA
u-op-30-mmea3	Cults Microwave support center	NA

Role Model: Organized Crime Members

Ref-Code	Name	Description
r-cm-1-mmea3	Bagman	NA
r-cm-2-mmea3	Capo crimine	NA
r-cm-3-mmea3	Capo di tutti capi	NA
r-cm-4-mmea3	Capodecina	NA
r-cm-5-mmea3	Caporegime	NA
r-cm-6-mmea3	Consigliere	NA
r-cm-7-mmea3	Crime boss	NA
r-cm-8-mmea3	Drug lord	NA
r-cm-9-mmea3	Gangster	NA
r-cm-10-mmea3	Gun moll	NA
r-cm-11-mmea3	Informant	NA
r-cm-12-mmea3	Made man	NA

r-cm-13-mmea3	Pentito	NA
r-cm-14-mmea3	Political boss	NA
r-cm-15-mmea3	Public enemy	NA
r-cm-16-mmea3	Russian Bratva Structure	NA
r-cm-17-mmea3	Soldato	NA
r-cm-18-mmea3	Thief in law	NA
r-cm-19-mmea3	Underboss	NA
r-cm-20-mmea3	Zips	NA

As a remark, the cult can have different role models, to serve different purposes. Business Analyst can extend the architecture by integrating other roles or units. For example, they can be perceived as mafia with the crime model, as terrorists with a terrorism model, and warriors with a military models. Depending what activities they are trying to have at different events. Sometimes they perform as criminals, sometimes they perform as terrorists, sometimes they perform as crusaders. No matter in what form, within this literature context, they are still harassment-centric.

Another remark is that hopefully readers can better understand cults by digesting the material inside the tables. To understanding cults is like understanding what a whole elephant is by touching its legs closing your eyes. Everyone can only understand part of it. This is why there are so many different tables, providing different views towards cults. The enterprise architecture model is to bring all the views and models together in a systematic and methodological way.

6 UNIT MODELS AND MECHANICS

Ref-Code	Models	Description
	First Principles	
	Basic communication model	
	Signal Interpretation	
	Criminal Profiling	
	Basic concepts of target programming (NLP)	
	Why cults prefer harassment centric models?	
	The Geographical Profiling Approach	

This section explains the basic mechanics and principles of harassment. We will introduce them from bottom up, in the two coming chapters, so that readers will have solid understand how harassment activities are engineered and every reader can devise solution specifically to their own case.

The First Principles

Harassment is that,

Ref-Code	Principles	Description
prin-1-mmea4	(1) An offender feeds signals to the target. Receiver takes the signals through sensory organs. After interpretation of the information, the Receiver feels uncomfortable.	NA

prin-2-mmea4	(2) The motives of harassment in the cults and communities context is that, the offender wants the receiver to change behavior through feeding stimulate signals. The changes would match offender's business goals, such as converting from non-cult to cult member, or to destroy non-cult rivalries.	NA
prin-3-mmea4	(3) In our context those signals are usually derogatory words or notes that would trigger receiver embarrassment or other uncomfortable feelings after interpretation.	NA
prin-4-mmea4	(4) "Intellect" Designers decide which signals are effective to each person, based on each person specific ways interpreting those words, that depend on target receiver's personal contextual information such as experience, character, history, or what the person has neural-linguistically programmed. For example, if the offender says word A to person A, person B is not likely to know offender is harassing person A, unless person B is aware of "word A" is a sensitive word to person A, and vice versa for person B.	NA
prin-5-mmea4	(5) Offenders first carry criminal profiling, so as to understand what stimuli would trigger what emotions to the target. They can design models and programs, through harassment events, to feed signals to the target, so that neuropaths can be programmed (deprogrammed).	NA
prin-6-mmea4	(6) After successful programming, the target change behavior, and their actions can be remotely controlled by the offenders. Offender can tell the target to do what ever the offender want. This process is known as conversion	NA

prin-7-mmea4	(7) The target can also be fed with large enough volume and intensity signals that psychological, psychiatrically, psychoneuroimmunologically, problems will get induced. This can drive target to severe depression, bipolar disorder, hallucinations, stress, trauma, and immune system breakdown.	NA
prin-8-mmea4	(8) Harassment is a preferred standard since it is hard for police to investigate and it is easier to implement than other offences, for example, car accidents, murders or rapes etc. Members are more willing to participate since they do not think harassment is illegal and punishment is enforceable. Also they recognize harassment a powerful sword that they can execute to any targets they want without criminal penalties.	NA

Basic communication model

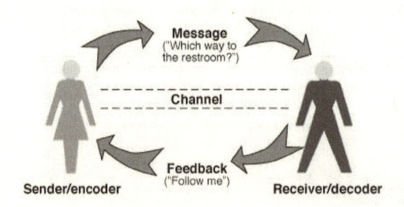

Fig 6-1. basic communication model (Smith, 2007)

The above is the basic and classic communication model between two objects, the target and receiver. This model is harassment neutral although harassment is based on communication. In harassment context sender is the offender, and receiver is the target. Message is words that trigger receiver emotion. Feedback can be verbal, facial or emotional expression. Sender would know right away if the stimuli were effective. (Smith, 2007)

Channels are diverse; we will enumerate all different channels they use later. For example, the channels are face-to-face, phone, email, talking behind you, yelling in front of you, interactive drama or trauma etc.

Signal Interpretation

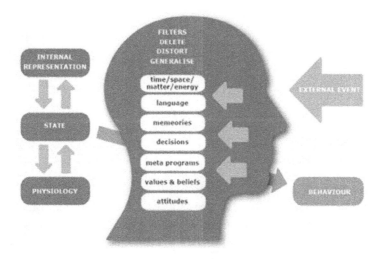

Fig 6-2. NLP Model (Fleming, Date)

This diagram explains how the receiver interpret the signals and give response.

The most important point here is that receiver can decide his/her way to interpret the signals, and he/she can decide how to behave after interpretation.

First the offender will feed a signal to the receiver. The tricky part here is the interpretation of the receiver. The offender consciously, unconsciously or subconsciously filters, delete, distort or generalize the signals.

The interpretation usually depends on the traits (physical state or situation (time/space/matter/energy), language, memories, decisions, meta programs, value and benefits and attitudes) of the receiver.

After interpretation of the signals, the receiver will or may change his/her emotion state from state 1 to state 2 (will discuss stateful harassment), present the interpretation internally, get the presentation neural programmed, and/or induce physiological actions (such damping immune system, hormones change) and behavioral responses.

For an experience offender or harassment designer, they are also professional programmer and manipulator. By profiling, they understand all the traits of the receiver. To meet professional standards, offender is aware of the harassment outcome (the behavior and what has been programmed) to the receiver, before signals are fed to receiver. The harassment or programming is considered to be successful, only if, the end results or responses from the receiver should match offender initial agenda.

Criminal Profiling

Initially criminal profiling is the process of inferring distinctive personality characteristics of individuals responsible for committing criminals act. (Turvey 2002: 1) (O'Connor, 2010 Aug 23).

"It is an attempt to provide investigators with more information on the offender who is yet to be identified." (Egger 1999: 243) (O'Connor, 2010 Aug 23).

However for cults and communities, profiling or criminal profiling, is the process of inferring distinctive personality characteristics of targeted individuals (new members, or rivalries) for offender's subsequent effective harassment act.

It is more effective to know ahead the target's emotional responses for each signal, before the cults and communities process any target. The below is a profile report template for basic profiling. (O'Connor, 2010 Aug 23 b)

Ref-Code	Attributes	Description
Prof-bas-1-mmea4	Salutation: To whom the report is written	NA
Prof-bas-2-mmea4	Opening paragraph: This could include a statement as to disorganized/organized offender type	NA
Prof-bas-3-mmea4	Target characteristics:	NA
Prof-bas-4-mmea4	Age	NA
Prof-bas-5-mmea4	Sex	NA
Prof-bas-6-mmea4	Race	NA
Prof-bas-7-mmea4	Intelligence	NA
Prof-bas-8-mmea4	Education	NA
Prof-bas-9-mmea4	Family/marital status	NA
Prof-bas-10-mmea4	Residence/living arrangements	NA
Prof-bas-11-mmea4	Vehicle type and condition	NA

Prof-bas-12-mmea4	Employment/occupation	NA
Prof-bas-13-mmea4	Psychosexual development/maturity level	NA
Prof-bas-14-mmea4	Provocation factors	NA
Prof-bas-15-mmea4	Interrogation recommendations	NA

Comprehensive Profile template (O'Connor, 2010 Aug 23 b)

Ref-Code	Attributes	Description
Prof-comp-A-mmea4	A. Inputs related to target lives	NA
Prof-comp-A.1-mmea4	1. Target lives scene video	NA
Prof-comp-A.2-mmea4	2. Target lives scene photographs	NA
Prof-comp-A.3-mmea4	3. Investigator's reports	NA
Prof-comp-A.4-mmea4	4. Target lives scene sketches	NA
Prof-comp-A.5-mmea4	5. Evidence logs and submission forms	NA
Prof-comp-A.6-mmea4	6. Results of all forensic analysis	NA
Prof-comp-A.7-mmea4	7. Medical examiner/coroner reports	NA
Prof-comp-A.8-mmea4	8. Autopsy photographs (wound patterns)	NA
Prof-comp-A.9-mmea4	9. Sexual assault protocol	NA
Prof-comp-A.10-mmea4	10. Written and taped statements of victims and witnesses	NA
Prof-comp-B-mmea4	B. Inputs related to victimology:	NA
Prof-comp-B.1-mmea4	1. Victim's lifestyle, friends, relatives	NA
Prof-comp-B.2-mmea4	2. Place of work and recreation	NA
Prof-comp-B.3-mmea4	3. Last known activities of victim	NA
Prof-comp-B.4-mmea4	4. Victim vulnerability and fantasy criteria	NA
Prof-comp-B.5-mmea4	5. Other symbolic criteria (why victim was selected)	NA
Prof-comp-B.6-mmea4	6. Points of contact (primary, secondary, intermediate)	NA
Prof-comp-C-mmea4	C. Inputs related to criminology of offender:	NA
Prof-comp-C.1-mmea4	1. Points of contact	NA
Prof-comp-C.2-mmea4	2. Disposal/dump site	NA

Prof-comp-C.3-mmea4	3. Method of approach (surprise/con/blitz)	NA
Prof-comp-C.4-mmea4	4. Method of attack (verbal/physical/from behind/with weapon or not)	NA
Prof-comp-C.5-mmea4	5. Method of control (striking/choking/binding/other restraints)	NA
Prof-comp-C.6-mmea4	6. Lethal force (controlling/punishing/sexual/size/weapons/fists)	NA
Prof-comp-C.7-mmea4	7. Weapons (kind/ownership/how transported/how used)	NA
Prof-comp-C.8-mmea4	8. Skill level of offender (signs of planning, precautionary measures	NA
Prof-comp-D-mmea4	D. Inputs related to victim/offender interaction:	NA
Prof-comp-D.1-mmea4	1. Victim compliance levels	NA
Prof-comp-D.2-mmea4	2. Victim resistance levels	NA
Prof-comp-D.3-mmea4	3. Signs of scripting	NA
Prof-comp-E-mmea4	E. Inputs related to *Modus Operandi*:	NA
Prof-comp-E.1-mmea4	1. Tools, vehicles, and equipment used	NA
Prof-comp-E.2-mmea4	2. Types of valuables/trophies/souvenirs taken	NA
Prof-comp-E.3-mmea4	3. Items used for restraint	NA
Prof-comp-E.4-mmea4	4. Lack of fingerprints or other evidence	NA
Prof-comp-E.5-mmea4	5. Wound patterns	NA
Prof-comp-E.6-mmea4	6. Signature behavior	NA
Prof-comp-E.7-mmea4	7. Signs of staging	NA
Prof-comp-F-mmea4	F. Inputs related to investigative strategy:	NA
Prof-comp-F.1-mmea4	1. Consistency/completeness of reports	NA
Prof-comp-F.2-mmea4	2. Case linkage	NA

Prof-comp-F.2.a-mmea4	a.	Behavioral dissimilarity (comparisons of two or more cases and they are not alike)	NA
Prof-comp-F.2.b-mmea4	b.	Investigative linkage (a general class connection between two or more cases)	NA
Prof-comp-F.2.c-mmea4	c.	Behavioral commonality (behavioral components have been compared are similar but not distinctive)	NA

After collecting information from victims, offenders are more confident harassing the targets or victims. The type of actions are programming (neuro-linguistic), paralyzing, and manipulation (remote control).

Basic concepts of target programming (NLP)

Step 1: dog—treat—> dog biscuits

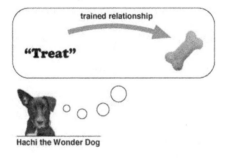

Fig 6-3. Training the dog (Smith, 2007b)

The following is an example on how an offender trains a dog. The end result is that the offender wants the dog to think about dog biscuits when he/she sends him verbal signal 'treat'. The dog will come over to the offender for biscuits (treat).

The offender trains the dog by presenting the biscuits to the dogs, while keep feeding the verbal signal, 'treats'. With time, an association will be developed between the sound 'treat' and the visual image 'biscuits'. Psychophysiologically, the neutral represents 'treat' and 'dog biscuits' are programmed inside the dog's mind.

Step 2: man—treat—> dog biscuits, derived relations dog biscuits—> treat

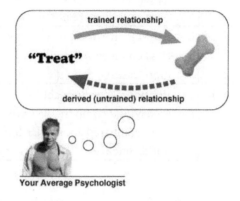

Fig 6-4. Training the man (Smith, 2007c)

If the trained object is smarter, he/she can derive a reverse association after being trained on the other side. That is when a dog biscuit is presented, he will think about the word 'treat' in his mind.

Step 3: train baby to derive reverse association

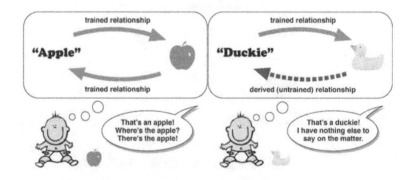

Fig 6-5. Training the baby (Smith, 2007d)

First train the baby the forward association between word 'apple' and the image apple. Second train the baby the reverse association, that is the image apple to the word 'apple'. Then the baby will gradually develop a sense that if A -> B, then B-> A (this is not a logic inference though). Then next time baby was trained.

Why cults prefer harassment-centric models?

Criminal cults offenders have been known to change or adjust their behavior in response to law enforcement action. Harassment Centric Enterprise Architecture is a conjecture of modeling their social behavior. The most powerful cults want to control everything, but not being too obvious that they are committing crimes. They are not physically killing or physical hurting people. They gradually and slowly corrode your mental health, hence making it hard for normal people to determine they have been hurt. Many cults members are white-collar professionals that they would prefer to integrate their knowledge and professions into mental conversion missions rather than physically hurting targets directly.

The Geographic Profiling Approach

A geographic profiling approach is useful because elements such as location and proximity are very important. Members enjoy 'Target and Hunt' that analysis of space or spatial factors (in criminal target patterns) is a quick way to get to the point. (O'Connor, 2010).

As a part of normal human behavior we have usual or typical environments (locations) in which we conduct our daily activities. These include our home and neighborhood, workplace, recreational sites, parking lots, bus stops, streets we travel between sites, and so forth

When an offender decides to obtain a victim he will carefully select those spaces in which he will operate according to his own criteria and needs. Just as the offender has spatial areas of choice, victims have areas of habit and comfort in which they live and operate. We call these activities 'target backcloth', and argues that because of this victim selection is mostly nonrandom, and it will require more specific behavioral activity on the part of the offender. (Rossmo, 2000)

7 SYSTEM MODELS

Now shift focus from operations to battlefields, i.e. Harassment-centric missions activities, events, and programs. These sections we have models describe how harassment programs are carried out at system level. Meaning multiple components, multi-units, multi-states etc.

Ref-Code	Models	Description
	Generic System Models	
	Causal Model	
	Spatial and temporal Model	
	Dynamic spatial Planning Model	
	Emotions Wheel Model	
	Profile Buzzwords Model—Emotion State Transitions	
	Multi-layer multi-state (MLMS) Process Model	
	Spatial-Process Integration Model	
	Redundancy Model—For Mission Critical Event	
	Sequence Diagram Model.	
	Harassment Roles Model	
	Implementation Models	
	Harassment-centric events and models in professional job search process (Implementation Model Example)	
	Harassment environment and Business Process—Understand the recruitment process.	

	Business Model—What can we do as a cult?	
	Scripting Model—Summary of Script	
	Cult Integration and Affiliation Models	
	Cloud Model	
	Cult Integration and Affiliation Model Architecture	
	Cults Integration Bus Architecture Model	
	Cults Integration, Network Server model	
	Multi-disciplinary end points Different connection, different drivers	
	Multi-disciplinary integration end points Enumeration (Advanced applied criminology)	
	Integration Operations and Units (Examples)	
	Cult Integration Maturity Model	
	Others	
	Cult Harassment Configuration Models	
	Harassment Configurations Signs and Enumerations	

Generic System Models

Causal Model

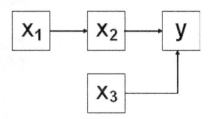

Fig 7-1. Basic Causal Model (von Lampe, 2003)

This model states cause and effect. X1 causes X2, X2 and X3 cause y.

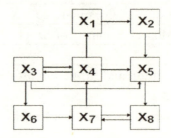

Fig 7-1. More complicated Analytic Causal Model (von Lampe, 2003)

The above is Causal analytic model of organized crime. There are bi-direction flows, loops between multiple causes and effects.

Spatial and temporal Model

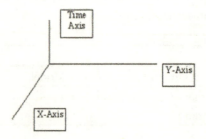

Fig 7-3. 3 dimensional spatial and temporal Model (Verma & Lodha, 2002)

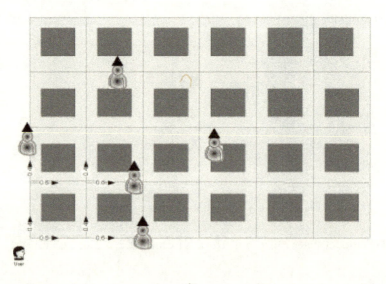

This is a 2 D grid of a street map. For users, each intersection there are probabilities of two possible paths to proceed. If I were the harasser, I would put my harassment troops at the most probable points and paths.

Dynamic spatial Planning Model

Now time is changing, troops have to move according in order to trespass in front of the target. t=0

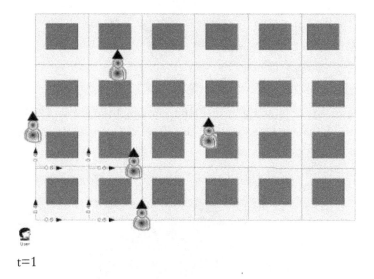

t=1

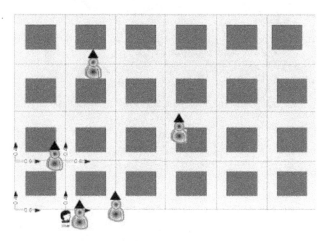

Troops move accordingly in order to trespass in front of the target.
t=3

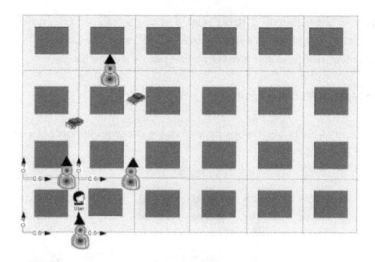

More cars come. Now the first offender has met the target. The offender is now chasing the target from behind. The target goes up, while the second and third offender is coming along.

Emotions Wheel Model

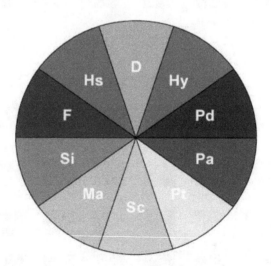

This is the emotion wheel. It can come as cycles or vicious cycles if appropriate harassment signals are fed to the target in each emotion state, triggering offender desired feeling. Target either gets converted for a relief, or continuous being manipulated to achieve different disorders at different states.

The above example has 10 states only. For clinical abnormal psychology, there are many more different states. It can be presented as DSM-IV manual. (as follows)

(O'Connor, 2010 Aug 23 c)

Ref-Code	types	description
Emo-dsm-axisI-mmea5	Axis I	Any disorder or condition other than personality disorders and mental Retardation
Emo-dsm-axisII-mmea5	Axis II	Personality disorders, mental retardation, and maladaptive defense mechanisms
Emo-dsm-axisIII-mmea5	Axis III	Medical conditions relevant to the case
Emo-dsm-axisIV-mmea5	Axis IV	Psychosocial and environmental problems,

Axis I Disorder (O'Connor, 2010 Aug 23 c)

Ref-Code	Types	Description
Emo-axisI-1 mmea5	Schizophrenia or other psychosis	NA
Emo-axisI-2 mmea5	Mood	NA
Emo-axisI-3 mmea5	Anxiety	NA
Emo-axisI-4 mmea5	Somatoform	NA
Emo-axisI-5 mmea5	Factitious	NA
Emo-axisI-6 mmea5	Dissociative	NA
Emo-axisI-7 mmea5	Sexual and Gender Identity	NA
Emo-axisI-8 mmea5	Eating or Sleep	NA
Emo-axisI-9 mmea5	Impulse control	NA
Emo-axisI-10 mmea5	Adjustment	NA
Emo-axisI-11 mmea5	Delirium and Amnesia	NA
Emo-axisI-12 mmea5	Others: Not Specified	NA

Axis II Disorder (O'Connor, 2010 Aug 23 c)

Ref-Code	Types	Description
Emo-axisII-1 mmea5	Paranoid	NA
Emo-axisII-2 mmea5	Schizoid	NA
Emo-axisII-3 mmea5	Schizotypal	NA
Emo-axisII-4 mmea5	Antisocial	NA
Emo-axisII-5 mmea5	Borderline	NA
Emo-axisII-6 mmea5	Histrionic	NA
Emo-axisII-7 mmea5	Narcissistic	NA
Emo-axisII-8 mmea5	Avoidant	NA
Emo-axisII-9 mmea5	Dependent	NA
Emo-axisII-10 mmea5	Obsessive-compulsive	NA
Emo-axisII-11 mmea5	Others: Not Specified	NA
Emo-axisII-12 mmea5	Mental retardation (IQ)	NA

MMPI (Minnesota Multiphasic Personality Inventory), as an Alternative of DSM-IV manual. (O'Connor, 2010 Aug 23 c)

Ref-Code	types	description
Emo-MMPI-1-mmea5	Hypochondriasis (Hs)	Bodily preoccupation
Emo-MMPI-2-mmea5	Depression (D)	Lacking in self confidence
Emo-MMPI-3-mmea5	Hysteria (Hy)	Psychosomatic symptoms
Emo-MMPI-4-mmea5	Psychopathic deviate (Pd)	Antisocial tendencies impulsive
Emo-MMPI-5-mmea5	Masculinity	Femininity (Mf) Sex
Emo-MMPI-6-mmea5	Paranoia (Pa)	Suspicious resentful
Emo-MMPI-7-mmea5	Psychasthenia (Pt)	Anxiety insecurity
Emo-MMPI-8-mmea5	Schizophrenia (Sc)	Bizarre thinking
Emo-MMPI-9-mmea5	Hypomania (Ma)	Excessive psychomotor activity
Emo-MMPI-10-mmea5	Social introversion (Si)	Shy
Emo-MMPI-11-mmea5	L scale	Need to give favorable impression
Emo-MMPI-12-mmea5	F scale	Pathological lying

Emo-MMPI-13-mmea5	K scale	Defensiveness
Emo-MMPI-14-mmea5	Fb scale	Inattention to some items
Emo-MMPI-15-mmea5	VRIN scale	Inconsistent responses
Emo-MMPI-16-mmea5	TRIN scale	Acquiescent responses

Regular-Non-clinical emotion state

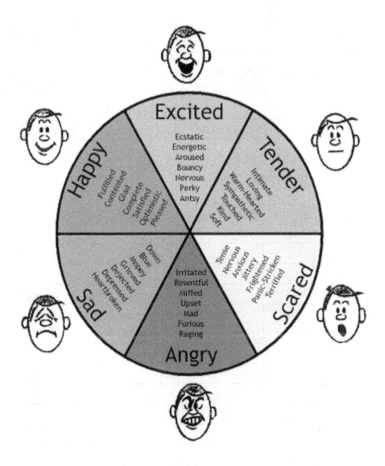

Fig 7-4 Emotion Wheel of regular emotion states

Profile Buzz words Model—Emotion State Transitions

After profiling, harassment leaders understand the target's emotional profile. Harassment offenders can feed different 'buzzwords' to control (State x) and manipulate (State x-State y) target's emotions.

Let us introduce this in a 4 states emotion cycle. Buzzwords can be a union or intersection of multiple buzzwords. Harassment profiler can put down N/A if information is not available.

State	State1	State2	State3	State4
State1	Buzzword 1	Buzzword 3	Buzzword 1 and Buzzword 4	Buzzword 3 or Buzzword 4 and Buzzword 5
State2	Buzzword 2	Buzzword 5 or Buzzword 4	Buzzword 5	Buzzword 1
State3	Buzzword 4	Buzzword 2	Buzzword 7 and Buzzword 4	Buzzword 4
State4	Buzzword 1	Buzzword 6	N/A	Buzzword 8

To expand it to a proper table format

Ref-Code	From State	To State	Relationship	Buzzwords
	1	1	1-1	Buzzword 1
	1	2	1-2	Buzzword 3
	1	3	1-3	Buzzword 1 and Buzzword 4
	1	4	1-4	Buzzword 3 or Buzzword 4 and Buzzword 5
	2	1	2-1	Buzzword 2
	2	2	2-2	Buzzword 5 or Buzzword 4
	2	3	2-3	Buzzword 5
	2	4	2-4	Buzzword 1
	3	1	3-1	Buzzword 4
	3	2	3-2	Buzzword 2
	3	3	3-3	Buzzword 7 and Buzzword 4
	3	4	3-4	Buzzword 4
	4	1	4-1	Buzzword 1
	4	2	4-2	Buzzword 6
	4	3	4-3	N/A
	4	4	4-4	Buzzword 8

Example: Substitute state {1,2,3,4} as state {happy, angry, sad, agitated}, and buzz word {1,2,3,4,5,6,7,8} as {apple, orange, egg, beef, soda, plane, hand, 'that is it'}. The table emerges as follows:

Ref-Code	From State	To State	Relationship	Buzzwords
	happy	happy	happy-happy	apple
	happy	angry	happy-angry	egg
	happy	sad	happy-sad	apple and beef
	happy	agitated	happy-agitated	Egg or beef and soda
	angry	happy	angry-happy	orange
	angry	angry	angry-angry	soda or beef
	angry	sad	angry-sad	soda
	angry	agitated	angry-agitated	apple
	sad	happy	sad-happy	beef
	sad	angry	sad-angry	orange
	sad	sad	sad-sad	hand and beef
	sad	agitated	sad-agitated	beef
	agitated	happy	agitated-happy	apple
	agitated	angry	agitated-angry	plane
	agitated	sad	agitated-sad	N/A
	agitated	agitated	agitate-agitated	"that's it"

So now the reader can visualize. This emotional profile can be purely profiled, or it can be artificially synthesized by neuro-linguistic programming (see section on harassment basic mechanics). After having finished feeding, usually offender would ask, "Do you have enough?", target may say, yes/no/too much or want to throw up, etc as a harassment manner. Clinically, if you do this too many times to your target, your target would have a mental or emotion breakdown. Also the magnitude of the signal strength also matters. If your target is getting weak after 'eating', it is time for the cult offender to 'save' them.

Multi-layer multi-state (MLMS) Process Model

Consider how human beings are more complex in reality, that it is very hard to change the behavior of a target.

For example, to convert a non-cult person to a cult member, to mentally and physically change certain behavior, such as locomotion to castle weekly, it has to go through a multi layer, multi state process.

Mental layer and physical layer have to coordinate. The motor output (Left, Right, Front), is driven by motor transitional signals (BC, BB, BE). The signals firing are from orders from the brain (cognitive map), only with mind state (BC, BB, BW). To get the mind cognitive signals fire to order locomotion, the brain has to go through paths in cognitive map, triggered by a motivation stimulus (M), going trough several mind states (CD—> CC->BC left, CD-CC->EC->EE->BE right, (BC && BB)—> BB front), plus the input of Transitions (CA) (BB,BC, BE). See the map below.

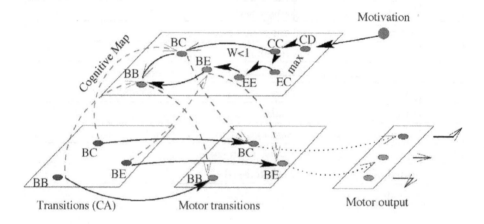

Fig 7-5. Interaction between the cognitive map and
the transitions (Cuperlier, Quoy and Gaussier, 2007).

Now consider that as a harassment programmer you have to program this to your target.

(M-CD-CC, CC-BC, CC-EC-EE-BE, BC+BE-> BB)

A Four processes Sequential Events

Ref-Code	Stage	Process	Diagram
	Stage 1	M-CD-CC	
	Stage 2	CC-BC	
	Stage 3	CC-EC-EE-BE	
	Stage 4	BC+BE-> BB	

How can we move them? Check the emotional profile, we have:

Ref-Code	From State	To State	Buzzwords	Role	
M	CD		Fire	Fireman	
CD	CC		Steam	Waterman	
CC	BC		"W > 1"	Monk	
CC	EC		"W < 1"	Monk	
EC	EE		Bake	Baker	
EE	BE		Stir	Stirrer	
BC && BE	BB		Fry && Bye	Monk	

See process Diagrams

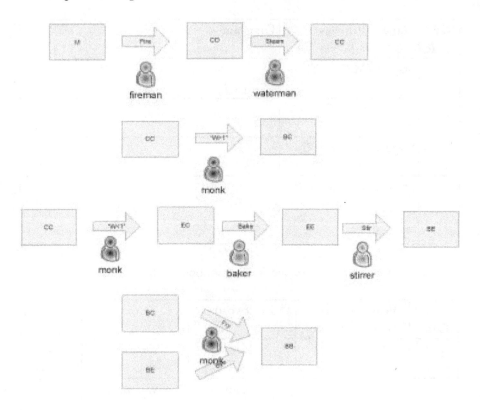

Spatial-Process Integration Model

Harassment leaders group these 4 processes into 2 events. Stage 1 and Stage 2 are in Markham event. Stage 3 and Stage 4 are in Richmond Hill event. In Event 1, we assign one fireman (fire) at (1,1) guarding the 1ˢᵗ street, the waterman (steam) at (2,2) guarding the 2ⁿᵈ street, and the monk (w>1) at (3,3) guarding the 3ʳᵈ street. The target's girl friend, Angie, is waiting for him to deliver flowers at (4,4). While target is walking towards (4,4), harassment troops are waiting for trespassing, stalking, and harassing him.

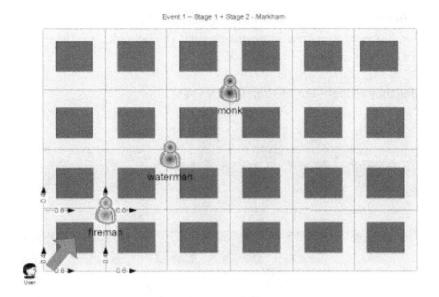

In Event 2, we assign one monk (w<1) at (1,1) guarding the 1st street, the Baker (bake) at (2,2) guarding the 2nd street, the stirrer (stir) at (3,3) guarding the 3rd street, and another monk at (4,4) guarding the 4th street. The target's bestfriend, Yuri, is waiting for him to eat together at (4,4). While target is walking towards (4,4), harassment troops are waiting for trespassing, stalking, and harassment him.

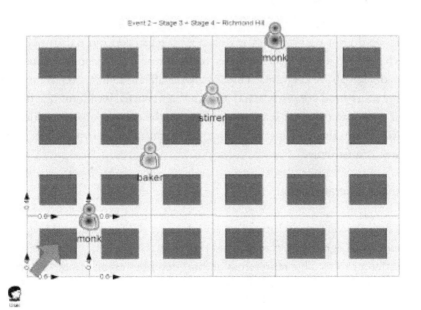

After this processes, I am sure the target would go to castle every week as a habit, just need to remind him perhaps (Evil Ha-ha). Otherwise he may get a mental disorder and go to hospital again.

Redundancy Model—For Mission Critical Event

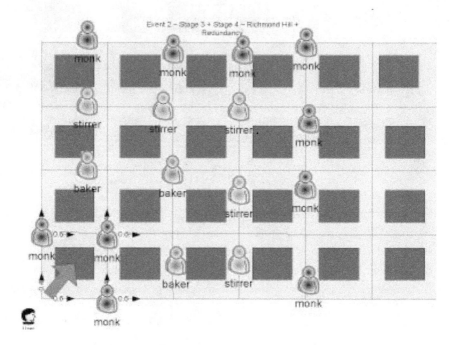

If we do not want to miss any chances, we can add more than one person in each role. No matter how the target walks, it would get trapped sequentially as planned. (See above diagram). The only trade off is the harassment unit has to prepare more head counts to stand by at different spatial locations. It is not a bad idea if manpower is not a scare resource, while the event is mission critical. Also you may group them to hurt the target together as an amplifying effect that can be more "constructive".

Sequence Diagram Model.

The following is a demonstration of using UML sequential diagram to represent the cognitive map events and processes. Notice the handshake between five different roles. This representation best describes asynchronous multi states event between different logic role units.

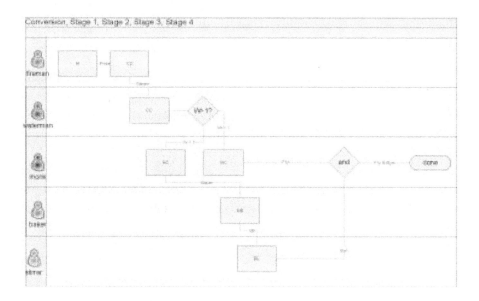

Harassment Roles Model

Ref-Code	Roles	Description
r-harass-1-emma5	Organizers	Core members who steer group
r-harass-2-emma5	Leadership—	Charismatic who lead group
r-harass-3-emma5	Communicators	Pass on directives
r-harass-4-emma5	Seconds in command	Pass on orders
r-harass-5-emma5	Intelligence	And counterintelligence agents
r-harass-6-emma5	Extenders	Recruiters of new members
r-harass-7-emma5	Bodyguards	Members who protect leaders
r-harass-8-emma5	Members	Those who do the harassment Operations—
r-harass-9-emma5	Sleepers	Members living under deep cover
r-harass-10-emma5	Insulators	Members who protect the core
r-harass-11-emma5	Guardians	Security enforcers
r-harass-12-emma5	Operations	Those who commit the harassment terror
r-harass-13-emma5	Financiers	Fund raisers & money Launderers
r-harass-14-emma5	Monitors	Advisors about group weaknesses
r-harass-15-emma5	Logistics	Keepers of safe houses
r-harass-16-emma5	Crossovers	People with regular jobs

Implementation Model Example—Harassment centric events and models in professional job search process

We are going to illustrate few more important system level harassment models, realizing another business use case, though a job search process example

Mission Statement: Stanley is in going through a transition in his career. He is looking for a new job. This is usually a stressful time and Stanley needs extra support. However, since he is not a cult member, it is a good opportunity for cult members to hurt him hard, make him collapse, and convert him afterwards. This time cult is leveraging its integration and penetration in the human resource, recruiting and professional community. It is time to get its massive crossovers and members involved in this mission.

Mission Target: To defeat Stanley during job search. Insult and make him feel he is useless, in a community public area (restaurant). We are going to leverage our deep penetration in job markets and professional communities. He is not going to live with dignity unless he get converted. We have to make Stanley feel like a loser.

Harassment environment and Business Process—Understand the recruitment process.

What can we do as a cult?

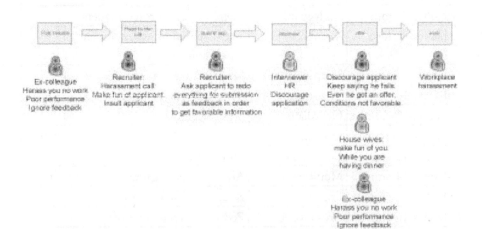

Summary of Script

Ref-Code	Stage in process	role	Communication channel	Script
	Post resume	Ex-colleague	F2F, feedback	"You suck." "You are a failure." "You are a loser." "You are not competent." "You do not fit the team."
	Head hunter call	Recruiter	Email, initiate conversation	"Can you give me a call?" "You have to call me if you want me to submit your resume."
	Head hunter call	Recruiter	Phone, harassment (avoid black and white)	"Are you currently employed?" "Why are you looking for a job?" "You have been out of work for few months already, you need to ask for less pay, in order to be competitive." "You are not competent enough to apply for this position." "Have you really been doing the stuff for 5 years?" "I do not think you are qualified, I can help you if you lower your rate." "We are the best recruiter in this area."

	Submit application	Recruiter	Email	Get everything from you for free. "Please redo your resume." (no further response) "Please provide me technical documents to prove you have done this." (no further response) "Please fill out all the matrixes." (no further response)
	No Interview	Recruiter	Email, phone	"Project on hold." "You suck.", "There are other better candidates." "Your previous employer says you suck."
	Interview	Interviewer HR	Face to face	"What is your last job rating?" "Why did you quit your job?" "How long have you been out of work?" "Why did you quit your second job? "Does not seem like you can perform." "You know what, You should beg your last employer to hire you back." "We do not think you can fit & qualify here." "Why don't you help yourself?" "Your last employer is a brilliant guy." "You know your last employer knows a lot people in the cult, perhaps you can ask him for mentorship."

	Fail Interview	Recruiter	Phone, email	"You failed/lost the interview" "Another candidate with half your price says he has 20 years experience." "You should think about adjusting your rate." "We have already helped you, but it does not seem to turn out that way." "Suddenly the company got a financial freeze, and they fired all contractors." "No response." "You should improve your communication."
	Fail Interview	Community House Wives.	Restaurants F2F harassment	"You suck." "You lose." "You fail the interview." "You perform poorly during the interview." "Your last employer says you have a poor attitude." (laughing) "You are unemployed." "You are useless." "After few months you are still unemployed." "My son just got promoted, he goes to cults activities every week." "You better join the cult, people there have better professional network." "You should have joined the cult earlier so you would not get kicked out from your last job." "You are fired."

	Fail Interview	Ex-Colleague (usually younger)	Restaurants F2F harassment	Crutches as "Feedback". "You have a poor rating every year", "You do not communicate well", "You are not a team player", "you do not have passion", "you do not align your goals with the senior management", "you are thinking of earning too much", "your work attitude is not good", "lucky we did not get kicked out this time, you are unlucky", "you just want to show off"
	Offer	Recruiter	Phone, email	Lower salary, title deflation, harsh and misleading conditions.
	Offer	Community House Wives.	Restaurants F2F harassment	"You make less than your last job." "You have title deflation." "You are no longer manager." "My son just got promoted as manager." "This is a new job, you have to start all over again from scratch, good luck." "Your last job was better, you should not have quit, even when they insulted you and compelled you to quit."

	Work	New Colleagues	Workplace F2F harassment	"Talk about your last boss." "Why did you leave your last boss?" "Feedback, you have communication problems." "You are not autonomous.", "You are not at par.", Get the buzzwords to wash you once in the first week as a warm welcome. "Can you be a team player?"
	Work	Community Housewives.	Restaurants F2F harassment	"You still suck." "You still lose." "You perform poorly still." "Your last employer tells your new employer you have a poor attitude." (laughing) "You will be unemployed." "You are useless." "After a few months you will be unemployed." "My son just got promoted in your last company, he goes to cult activities every week and he makes everyone happy." "You better join the cult, they have better professional network." "You should have joined the cult earlier so you would not get kicked out of your job." "You will be fired if you do not surrender"

	Work	Ex-Colleagues	Restaurants F2F harassment	"We are so busy." "He just got promoted." "Poor communication." "You are not a loyal person." "Only we can deliver patents and publications." "What company is this? Never heard about it." "How much are you making now?" "We feel very proud working in a blue chip company, so do you?" "I am still in company XX."

These are what people say routinely during career transition process. After a few iterations you will find them mechanical, and you may think they are just performing their routine duties as cult members. Some people need to say this in order to sustain themselves.

Cult Integration and Affiliation Models

Problem Statement: How can we connect to relevant people and get them engaged in this mission?

The Integration and Affiliation Model illustrates how cults penetrate to different units in the mainstream society. Cults get themselves socially integrated to social units such as companies, government ministries, senates, professional chapters and public utilities, as an infrastructure development and extension.

With this integration, they can control and manipulate operations belong to the society at large. This integration is multipurposes, such as,

Cults want to have a social impact through implementing a wheel of disasters.

Cult leaders want to manipulate certain non-members outside the cult's circle to deliver the message that they are everywhere, by coordinating with members to harass non-members in socially penetrated units.

Cults want to perform social marketing through manipulating and leveraging public utilities such as mass media and public utilities.

Get funding from companies, while cults provide a kind of 'social support' to business units.

So how can we use the models?

Stanley's boss, Erik is a cult member and has been pushing Stanley to contribute to the cult in order to keep his job. Stanley did not give him a shit so Erik tortures him till he quit. Erik actually escalated Stanley's problem to a cult priest Rotan to make sure Stanley would face on-going misfortunes in other workplaces, if he continues refusing to join cult.

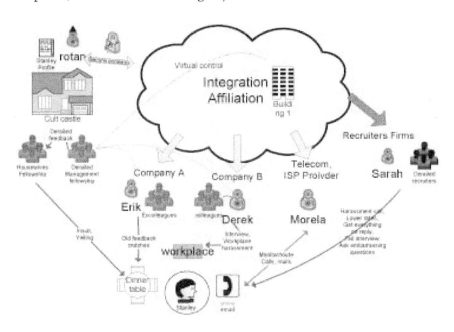

Cloud Model

In order to implement this, you need external support to the cult. Erik (Company A) talks to Rotan. Rotan coordinates and communicates through Integration & Affiliate networks. Rotan communicates with Derek and team (Company B, Stanley's destination company), Morela (Telecommunication company), Sarah and other recruiters (recruiter firms). Rotan delegates the harassment activities to two cult fellowships, 'derailed management fellowship', and 'Housewives love & care Fellowship' as the harassment operations for this mission. Rotan pulls out the criminal profile of Stanley and passes it to the operations. Erik from company A also brings out Stanley's ex-colleagues as a support operation for harassment.

To explain the division of labor, first Morela's job here is to monitor Stanley's emails and phone calls and route them to recruiter teams. Recruiter teams will harass Stanley using the phone, based on the monitored information and command sent by derailed management operations. Sarah is the main recruiter contact of the Company B job Stanley has. The recruiters groups will keep Stanley job application kinky and discouraging throughout the process. When Stanley gets to an office location for an interview or other hands-on tasks, Derek, the assigned manager in company B, will embarrass Stanley during the interview or stress him out using feedback, while he is reported to the derailed management team from the cult. When Stanley gets discouraged, he will go out to have dinner, Rotan and the derailed management fellowship will send troops (housewives love and care and his ex-colleagues from Company A) to further spit on Stanley. Stanley 's wheel of negative emotions turns like crazy, and probably he will be converted after a few stressful iterations.

Cult Integration and Affiliation Model Architecture

So what is inside the clouds? This section talk about what and how cults get integrated with other pieces.

Principle: Any operation and unit in the public or private sectors can be intergrated or affiliated, as end-points, as long as cults as a unit have any access control or influence, mostly without ownership. (If they have ownership, the operation will be the cults property, not integration end-points.

Cults Integration Bus Architecture Model

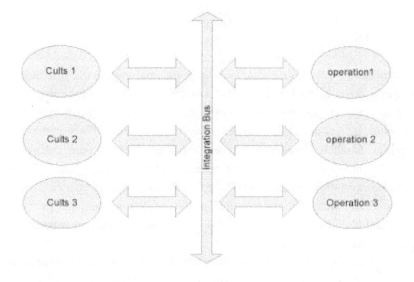

On the highest level there is a group of cults, sharing the same integration bus, talking to operations (operation 1, operation 2, operation 3). The integration bus can be treated as the common communication platform between groups of cults, to groups of social operations.

Cults Integration, Network Server model

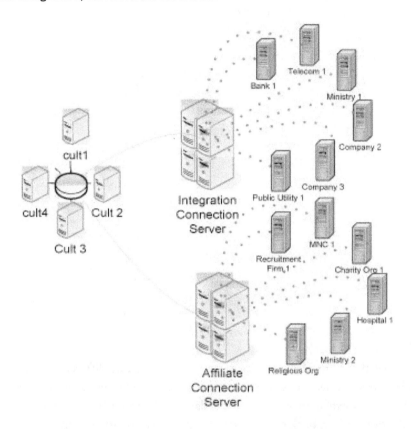

The bus is actually an infrastructure, which is hosted by connection servers, (Integration and affiliate connection servers). Connection servers are hub that route request from cults servers to the operation servers. Notice there are different kinds of end-point servers, (such has Bank 1, Telecom 1 Ministry 1, Company 2, Company 3, Recruitment Firm 1, Religious Organization). Different application servers represent different business function operations. The connection server can connect to diverse sets of multi-disciplinary servers to deliver certain functions, without having total ownership of them. With this integration, the cult functionality can be extended.

Multi-disciplinary end-points: Different connections, different drivers

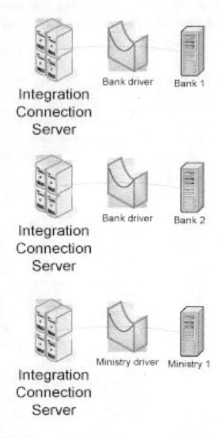

Since there are many different kinds of endpoints, different connections needs different drivers to connect to different end-points, using different sets of protocol, contextual information, meta-data etc. For bank 1 and bank 2, we can use the same driver, bank driver. Each end-point has to install a driver in order to talk to a connection server and cult servers.

What are the lower level protocols and contextual information underneath? In this literature we are trying to keep integration abstract that details would be hidden. However, you can think of sending people to the operation and operate, establishing mutual agreement, and mutual support etc as integration lower level mechanics.

Multi-disciplinary integration end-points: Enumeration (Advanced applied

criminology) (O'Connor, 2010 Aug 23 c).

Ref-Code	Types	Description
appcrim-1-emma5	Medicine	Natural illness
appcrim-1-emma5	Psychiatry	Mental illness
appcrim-1-emma5	Psychoanalysis	Unconscious guilt/defense mechanisms
appcrim-1-emma5	Sociology	Learning from bad companions
appcrim-1-emma5	Anomie	State of normlessness/goal-means gap
appcrim-1-emma5	Differential Opportunity	Absence of legitimate opportunities
appcrim-1-emma5	Alienation	Frustration/feeling of being cut off from others
appcrim-1-emma5	Identity	Hostile attitude/crisis/sense of sameness
appcrim-1-emma5	Identification	Making heroes out of legendary criminals
appcrim-1-emma5	Containment	Outer temptation/inner resistance balance
appcrim-1-emma5	Behavior Modification	Reward/Punishment Programming
appcrim-1-emma5	Social Defense	Soft targets/absence of crime prevention
appcrim-1-emma5	Guided Group Interaction	Absence of self-responsibility/ discussion
appcrim-1-emma5	Interpersonal Maturity	Unsocialized, sub-cultural responses
appcrim-1-emma5	Sociometry	One's place in a group network system
appcrim-1-emma5	Dysfunctional Families	Members 'feed off' other's neurosis
appcrim-1-emma5	Control Theory	Weak social bonds/natural predispositions
appcrim-1-emma5	Strain Theory	Anger, relative deprivation, inequality
appcrim-1-emma5	Subcultures	Criminal values as normal within group
appcrim-1-emma5	Labeling Theory	Self-fulfilling prophecies/name-calling
appcrim-1-emma5	Neutralization	Self-talk, excuses before behavior
appcrim-1-emma5	Drift	Sense of limbo/living in two worlds

appcrim-1-emma5	Reference Groups	Imaginary support groups
appcrim-1-emma5	Operant Conditioning	Stimuli-to-stimuli contingencies
appcrim-1-emma5	Reality Therapy (1965	Failure to face reality
appcrim-1-emma5	Gestalt Therapy (1969	Perception of small part of 'big picture'
appcrim-1-emma5	Transactional Analysis (1961	No communication between inner parent-adult-child
appcrim-1-emma5	Biodynamics (1955	Lack of harmony with environment
appcrim-1-emma5	Nutrition and Diet (1979	Imbalances in mineral/vitamin content
appcrim-1-emma5	Metabolism (1950	Imbalance in metabolic system
appcrim-1-emma5	Biofeedback (1974	Involuntary reactions to stress
appcrim-1-emma5	Biosocial Criminology (1977	Environment triggers inherited 'markers'
appcrim-1-emma5	The 'New Criminology' (1973	Ruling class oppression
appcrim-1-emma5	Conflict Criminology (1969	Structural barriers to class interests
appcrim-1-emma5	Critical Criminology (1973	Segmented group formations
appcrim-1-emma5	Radical Criminology (1976	Inarticulation of theory/praxis
appcrim-1-emma5	Left Realism (1984	Working class prey on one another
appcrim-1-emma5	Criminal Personality (1976	53 errors in thinking
appcrim-1-emma5	Criminal Pathways Theory (1979	Critical turning/tipping points in life events
appcrim-1-emma5	Feminism (1980	Patriarchal power structures
appcrim-1-emma5	Low Self Control Theory	Impulsiveness, Sensation-seeking
appcrim-1-emma5	General Strain Theory	Stress, Hassles, Interpersonal Relations

Integration Operations and Units (Examples)

Ref-Code	Types	Description
	Publication	NA
	Television	NA
	Workplace	NA
	Telecommunication	NA
	Satellite	NA
	Transportation	NA
	Companies	NA
	Street Troops	NA
	Schools & Colleges	NA
	Casinos	NA
	Relaxation Facilities	NA
	Weapons & Army	NA
	Agriculture Area	NA
	Chemicals	NA
	Pharmaceutical	NA
	Infrastructure	NA
	Animal	NA
	Troops	NA
	Supermarket	NA
	Base	NA
	Theater	NA
	Financial	NA
	Department	NA
	Radio Station	NA
	Factories	NA
	Technology Lab	NA
	Nuclear Plant	NA
	Hospital	NA
	Secret Buddhist Temple	NA
	Pyramid	NA
	Plant	NA
	Multinational Corporation	NA

	Cabinet	NA
	Restaurant / Public Place	NA
	Elderly	NA
	Family / Domestic	NA
	Job Search	NA
	Medical	NA
	Public Utility	NA
	Sexual & Racial	NA
	Religious Organization	NA
	Goggle / Search Engine Company	NA
	Information Technology	NA
	Commercial	NA
	Vehicles	NA

Community Integration Maturity Model

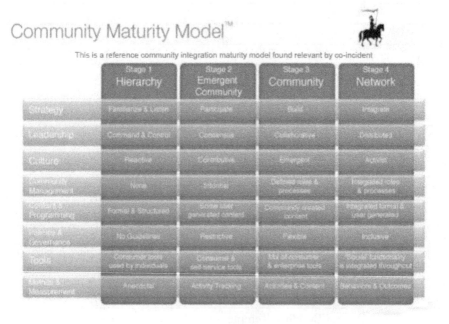

Fig 7-6. community integration maturity mode (Happe 2009)

System Configurations

Cult Harassment Configuration Models

Problem Statement: From the above example, Stanley is going to restaurants and get harassed. This is different now than trespassing on the street blocks. Stanley is not moving now; he is sitting in the middle of the restaurants. What would be the configuration representation if he is in the restaurant? Besides walking on the street and eating restaurant, are there any other scenarios that we need other configuration models?

Dinner Table configuration

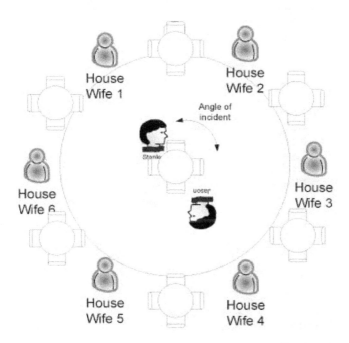

Stanley gets his best friends Jason to a Japanese restaurant. Somehow there are 6 housewives sitting around him in six directions. They are talking agitatedly to each other. They have glasses and their mouths are big.

Script: Event: Stanley, Jason at Japanese restaurants. '360 degree' feedback, taken care by housewives.

Ref-Code	Role	Script
	Housewife 1	"Lost job", "Sorry", "Lost job", "Chicken Teriyaki."
	Housewife 2	"Should have listened to Erik's feedback."
	Housewife 3	"You know my daughter is working as a manager under Erik."
	Housewife 4	"That guy has a very poor working attitude, not talking about you sorry."
	Housewife 5	"I am going to lunch tomorrow with Derek. He told me he has just interviewed a mentally retarded guy."
	Housewife 6	"That guy probably has poor luck these days. He should pray and come and join us."

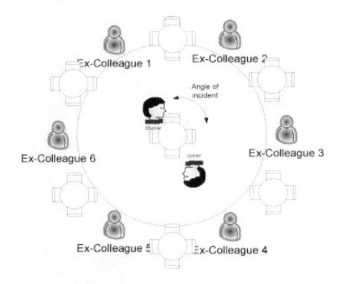

Script: Event: Stanley, Jason at sports Bar. '360 degree' feedback, taken care by Stanley's Company A ex-colleagues.

Ref-Code	Role	Script
	Ex-colleague 1	"You suck." "Lost again."
	Ex-colleague 2	"Losers, Losers, not talking about you small BJ."
	Ex-colleague 3	"Ha ha, this guy, poor attitude, no work."
	Ex-colleague 4	"Ha ha, I just got promoted."

	Ex-colleague 5	"His skillset is too low for Company B."
	Ex-colleague 6	"We are the best, no MR person likes small BJ."
	Jason	"Join us on Sunday." "Beg your boss to rehire you."

Other interesting scripts

Ref-Code	Plot	Roles	Script
	Erik knows Stanley is applying for a job in Company B	Erik-Rotan	Erik: Stanley is going to apply for a job in Company B. Rotan: We have another opportunity. I want him to lose confidence. This time he must surrender Let me coordinate things for you
	Erik got hooked up with Derek	Erik-Derek	Erik: Can you take care of Stanley? This guy sucks, This guy stinks.
	Erik and Derek got hooked up with Sarah	Derek-Sarah	Derek: Sarah, can you make Stanley's rate to be $10? Can you ask Stanley how long have he been out of work? Can you ask Stanley to fix his resume 10 times before submission?
	Sarah get feedback to Stanley	Sarah-Stanley	Sarah: The client says you are not a good fit. Project has no funding.
	Erik reinforces his thought about Stanley to Derek	Erik-Derek	Erik: Thank you Derek. Thank you so much. This guy hurt us a lot and ruined our image. You know what? He should come on Sunday. We have social workers to change his attitude.
	Derek's reply to Erik	Derek-Erik	Sure, no problem. By the way, thanks for hiring my son last summer, he is graduating from Waterloo in June . . . Are you guys hiring in company A?
	Erik's reply to Derek	Erik-Derek	Please submit resume to HR first. I will take care of it. Me and other cult fellowship members are all hiring managers. Your son should be fine.

Harassment Configurations Signs and Enumerations

Ref-Code	Item	Sign	Description
conf_ sign-1-emma5	Signal		Harassment or other signals. It can be positive, negative, and other. Use different colors and labels to differentiate the nature of signals.
conf_ sign-2-emma5	Incumbent, high level harassment indication		Target is situated in an abstract harassment environment (platform neutral).
conf_ sign-3-emma5	Street walkers trespassing		Stalkers trespass on the street to harass targets, walking.
conf_ sign-4-emma5	Car trespassing, crashing		Trespass and stalk using cars. Can implement car crash.
conf_ sign-5-emma5	Oven, broadcast		Cults leader harass target in front of the public using broadcast engines, microphones or mass media.
conf_ sign-6-emma5	Harass within vehicle		Harass target inside the vehicle chamber, usually during a trip
conf_ sign-7-emma5	Dinner table harassment		Have dinner with and get harassed by Cult friends and relatives. Usually in feeding mode.
conf_ sign-8-emma5	System level, multiple dinner table harassment		Your dinner table is okay. But stalkers harass you and your friends from other tables, carrying individual conversation with buzzwords.
conf_ sign-9-emma5	Synchronization Stalking		Stalk and trespass, using telecommunication time and space synchronization through mob-like devices. Need social integration with telecommunication companies.

conf_ sign-10-emma5	Home office harassment		Stalkers use incoming calls, electronic messages, cyber harassment, house trespassers and other means to get you to feel they are everywhere, even when you are hiding inside your house.
conf_ sign-11-emma5	9-square fly star configuration		Metaphysical configuration. Stalk and harass from nine different directions. Target cognitively gets different uncomfortable feelings from different angles of penetration.
conf_ sign-12-emma5	Harassment Wheel		It can be a wheel of emotions, wheel of disasters, wheel of unfortunate events, wheel of agitations, depending on the sign label specification. Target just gets a feeling of spinning emotionally or psychotically and feels crazy.
conf_ sign-13-emma5	Adaptive, JIT (Just in time), harassment.		Kind of cyber harassment. Targets cyber activities get stalked. Human intervention or artificial automation feedback available. Can drive target crazy if he computer feed him news with buzzwords he typed or from cult's criminal profiling. Need cults penetration on ISP or websites companies.

conf_ sign-14-emma5	Social Network harassment		System level harassment, harassing target's social network first, such as family, friends, work colleagues, relatives, alumni, etc. After being able to control target's network, manipulators can manipulate or hurt target indirectly by sending signals to network members. These can be hearing bad news about your friends and family, or your network members come back to target and hurt target. Usually this is for hurting target who cannot be hurt directly, also it is more worthwhile to convert people around him first, if others are easier to convert. Graph theory or social network models can be applied here to explain the mechanics, which is not going to cover in this edition.

8 PUBLIC MODELS

Cults perceive themselves as sovereign, and it is necessary for a sovereign to have public administration tools, mass media penetration, and political/public policy influences. In order to achieve these privileges, this cult has to be maturely developed, highly integrated and penetrated into different public and private sector units. The penetration is so deep and so broad that even the real sovereign government is afraid of going against the cult directly.

A mature cult never commits crimes directly. They just motivate others to do what they want, usually hurting themselves at the same time. Patterns observed reveal that they are the ultimate benefactors after all the disasters, tragedies, mysterious events happened. Units, including government may get into deep trouble or scandals if they have once displeasing them.

Naturally people who execute those events get caught and punished. There is no solid proof against them having organized things in the background. However, interestingly you can see cult members feel very glad and proud as a result of those things having happened.

These all are motivations for writing this section. However, those phenomena are too hard to investigate. This section would introduce some relevant public administration models, assuming they have the ominous power of manipulating public affairs as a fact, and how the cult owner can leverage this to achieve his commercial goals.

Public Administration as Corporate Strategies

Think you are the highest enterprise strategy planner of the cult. You have the power to manipulate public affairs. You want to align organization benefits to what you impact on society, or vice versa, i.e. align social impact to the benefit of your organization.

A successful strategy has to consider: (1) People Satisfaction, (2) Customer Satisfaction, (3) Impact on Society, and (4) Benefits to Organization.

It has to be a win-win situation, that goals from all four dimensions align with each other. For example, cult owners want to create social events, or movements that would create new business opportunities, change the public behavior and perspective that, joining cults is an obligation socially and culturally, or at least it is commercially cool to join cults. The public will feel guilty if they do not join cults.

You can perceive that all these harassment-centric social movement are social marketing and social programming ventures to change public behavior towards cults as a commercial product.

The harassment-centric (buzzwords on dummies) social marketing and programming model would be the main theme in this section. Other models are regular public administration models that support cult social marketing.

Ref-Code	Perspective	Description
strat-1-emma06	Organization vision:	- Integrate fully with society. - Social Movements: Promoting cults trough 'Enterprise Risk Management Integration' program, and 'We are everywhere program.' - Goal 1: Lots of cults members become decision makers, executives, and senior management in private and public sectors. - Goal 2: Tremendous funding from enterprises, public and political sectors. Cults provide 'social and community support' to enterprises. Enterprises provide financial support and get more cult members into decision-making position as a return favor. Added values are shared between cults and organizations. - Tools: Harassment-centric campaigns at public level. It is natural as the prime theme of cult is harassment-centric activities. Cult members have track records of successfully achieving goals using harassment-centric events.

strat-2-emma06	Social Impact:	- Lots of catastrophic, scandal and disastrous events, especially to operations, which have never cared much about cults Mysterious wars, disasters, riots, scandals, accidents happen, especially to people who do not support cults. - The public will gradually get converted, just by watching the news everyday, subconsciously aware that they are all carried out by cults, thinking that supporting cults is the only solution, otherwise they will get into similar troubles. - To the wider public, the programs deliver a message that if operations and companies cooperate with cults, fortunes befall, else wheel of disasters comes into play. - Support the cults, life will be smooth, prosperous, healthy, or else kinks, not healthy, no prosperities, tragedies etc. Social behavioral change towards cults will come about after a while.
strat-2-emma06	Customer Satisfaction:	- If organization accepts the full enterprise risk management package from cults, no disasters will happen, otherwise disasters will happen. Customer are very happy funding the cults and hiring cult members since nothing bad happened after getting integrated with the cults. - The package includes: * Get cults members into board of directors, decision-making and other management positions. * Donate lumpsum to cults as community charity involvement fund. * Professional members of the cult would recommend companies to engage a portfolio of risk management programs, such as integrating risk management effort to enterprise level, risk outsource program, insurance program, reorganizing capital structures and other corporate resources. * Companies will get ongoing support by cults. They will protect the running businesses. Nothing wrong will happen since the 'community' will take care of them.

strat-2-emma06	People (Cult Member) Satisfaction:	- Only our members can get into high rank, high salary positions. - Kids of parents who join cults have jobs, those while kids of those parents who do not join cults do not have jobs. - Even members who do not have formal organization jobs, can participate in community harassment program, such as 'we are everywhere' program and 'wheel of disasters realization' programs. Since those programs are well-funded, members can support themselves during transitions. - Some other members can perform as professional problem-solvers on the other hand to their companies. Companies are happy to pay them money if they can work out plans with disasters implementation teams so that companies who pay would not get hurt.

Regular Public Administration Models

Catastrophic Events Categorization Model

Ref-Code	Channel	Description	Example
crisis-1-emma6	Hazard (notification)	Specify the cause of emergency	Natural Disasters, Accidents (Unintentional), Terrorism (Intentional)
Crisis-2-emma6	Peril (notification)	Specify the type of threatening event or phenomenon	Blast, Fire, Hazard Materials, Flooding, Tsunami, Land Slide, Avalanche
crisis-3-emma6	Coping Behavior-Evacuation (notification)	Specify the type of behavior to evacuate from the peril	Horizontal move, Vertical move, No move
crisis-4-emma6	Coping Behavior-Sheltering (notification)	Specify the type of place people will stay for their safety	Public Shelter, Shelter-in-place, Open place, Meeting Point

crisis-5-emma6	Location (notification)	Specify the way of notifying people the potential threat at site and appropriate safety actions to be taken in case	Pictograms, Signs, Warning statement, Map, Electronic Text Message
crisis-6-emma6	Timing (Alert)	Specify the way and criterion to alert people to seek additional information	Sound, light, color

Lievrouw and Finn's Communication Models

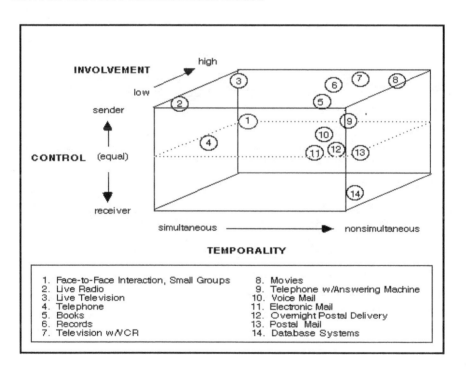

Fig 8.2 Lievrouw and Finn's Communication Models (Thomlison, 2000)

Ref-Code	Channel	Involvement (low, high)	Control (sender, receiver)	Temporality (simultaneous, no simultaneous)
comm-1-emma6	Face to Face Small Groups	High	Equal	Simultaneous
comm-2-emma6	Live Radio	Low	Sender	Simultaneous
comm-3-emma6	Live Television	High	Sender	Simultaneous
comm-4-emma6	Telephone	Middle	Equal	Simultaneous
comm-5-emma6	Books	Low	Sender	Non-Simultaneous
comm-6-emma6	Records	Low	Sender	Non-Simultaneous
comm-7-emma6	Television w/VCR	High	Sender	Non-Simultaneous
comm-8-emma6	Movies	High	Sender	Non-Simultaneous
comm-9-emma6	Telephone / Answering Machine	High	Equal	Non-Simultaneous
comm-10-emma6	Voice Mail	Middle	Equal	Non-Simultaneous
comm-11-emma6	Electronic Mail	Low	Equal	Non-Simultaneous
comm-12-emma6	Overnight Postal Delivery	Low	Equal	Non-Simultaneous
comm-13-emma6	Post Mail	Low	Equal	Non-Simultaneous
comm-14-emma6	Database System	Low	Receiver	Non-Simultaneous

Cult Public Administration Channel Model

Ref-Code	Public Administration Channels	Examples	Description
chann-1-emma6	Mass media News	National television channels, National radio stations, National broadcasting media, National wide newspaper / publication.	Cults can create news events through the realization of wheel of misfortunes. This includes catastrophic events, disasters, terrorisms, scandals etc through harassment-centric manipulation, organized or motivated by cults. Cults want to use mass media news to bring out some messages favorable to them.
chann-2-emma6	Mass media general	Magazines, Journals, non—news mass media programs.	Cults can create entertaining harassment events to celebrities or public figures, so as to bring propaganda messages such as "they can be everywhere" and "they can make your life entertaining."
chann-3-emma6	Catastrophic Events Trigger	Terrorism, Wars, Riots, Fire, Plant Explosion	Using, motivating or sponsoring terrorism and criminal organizations affiliates. Cults have lots of talented professionals that can provide knowledge on implementing those events flawlessly so as not to get into trouble.

chann-4-emma6	Regional Riots Trigger	Jasmine Revolution	Contact local activates through internet social networking tools and groups. Advisory support for propaganda, riot events organization, how to get around the police etc. A riot can trigger bloody events, revolution or civil war. Those events would be broadcast through mass media news.
chann-5-emma6	Community Radio Station and other broadcasting events	Local programs, commentaries, comedies etc.	Public utility is not owned by cults, but integrated with cults. Cult members can join the programs to express their opinion on public and entertainment affairs from their perspective. They are not necessary cult programs but they have to present programs in a way that cult member would not get emotionally triggered. They are mostly pro-cults.
chann-6-emma6	Public Programs, Social movement	Riots, Public live drama program, Social Marketing and programming	Can be bloody or emotionally/mentally harmful to public. This is to impact the society at a deeper level. Those events would get broadcasts through news. These programs have been well-known for its negative impact on public welfare, public health, and national security.

chann-7-emma6	Scandals Implementation	Public figures, politician, head of organization Scandals	Bring Scandals to their rivals. Get them embarrassed in the public and shared by everyone in the public. Can bring political opportunities to cults penetration if those leaders have been politically savvy enough to suppress cults actions
chann-8-emma6	Charity Events and Campaigns	Donation to Tsunami, and other disasters	Build-up positive image. Build rapport with charity organizations, and political organizations handling charity events. Sometimes cults are also implementer or motivator of the disasters.
chann-9-emma6	Elections Campaigns	Put cults members in elections.	Cults put a lot of members in regional and provincial elections and ensure their victory using population. They black mouth political rivalries that discourage the social movement of cults. Cults also sponsor and boost favorable political parties.
chann-10-emma6	Propaganda implementation	Cults publication. Public illusion, Communication error, evasion	They can use their public administration vehicles, just to hurt a person, or to evade a problem, by stirring things up, lying, exploit hates, brainwashing, keeping on broadcasting something wrong etc.

chann-11-emma6	Lobbying	Public Policy Intervention	They can use their formal or informal political influence to public policy decision makers and legislators to make favorable policies. They would harass decision makers if decisions are not favorable enough.
chann-12-emma6	Cult-specific newspapers and publications	To hate a person, express their opinions on social events	Usually full of emotions and hate, and most of the time, different than the majority public. They can say whatever they want. Many items are said at the community level and they serve as platform for cult members to express themselves.
chann-13-emma6	Internet Social networking applications	Facebook, twitter, groups and events Linkedin, public forums	Very popular tools to organize riots and revolution. Cults are good at facilitating these, and give treats to sovereign.

Stages Model

How cult introduces a social change step by step, starting from sponsoring Film or media project?

Ref-Code	Stage	Description
Stage-1-emma6	Quality File, Media Project	Movie 'wheel of disasters'. All the electronic compliances at home are out of control. They become individuals and mess things up. Lots of catastrophic events get broadcasted.

Stage-2-emma6	Increase in Public Awareness	Cults are everywhere. Shock Therapy. Companies and households need to manage their risks, accept cult's service in order to live peacefully.
Stage-3-emma6	Increased Public Engagement	Social Integration. Get cult members to chair social or community committees. Cults start to share value with community.
Stage-4-emma6	Stronger Social Movement	Riots, wars, accidents, assignations, scandal, terrorism.
Stage-5-emma6	Social Change	If we join cults, wheel of fortunes; If we do not join cults, wheel of misfortune. We better join cults if we want to survive.

Smart Power equalizer Model

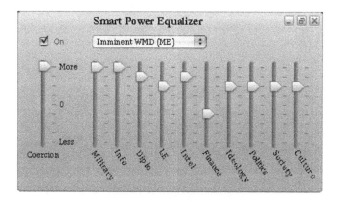

Fig 8-3. Smart Power Equalizer (Armstrong 2007)

This model quantifies each public vehicle. The quantity needed for each item is slightly adjustment-based on current situation. Seems that in the example, more military and international diplomacy are needed. Information and Intelligence are in high demand to support military action.

Ref-Code	Stage	Description	Coercion
poweq-1-emma06	Military	Military	5 + (lot more)
poweq-1-emma06	Info	Information	5 + (lot more)
poweq-1-emma06	Diplo	Diplomacy	4 + (quite a loft more)
poweq-1-emma06	L.E.	L.E. (Legal?)	3 + (more)

poweq-1-emma06	Intel	Intelligence	4 +
poweq-1-emma06	Finance	Finance	2 − (slightly less)
poweq-1-emma06	Ideology	Ideology	3 + (more)
poweq-1-emma06	Politics	Politics	3 + (more)
poweq-1-emma06	Society	Society	3 + (more)
poweq-1-emma06	Culture	Culture	3 + (more)

Multi Tier Social Units Model—Government, Public Affairs/ Policies, Media, Public

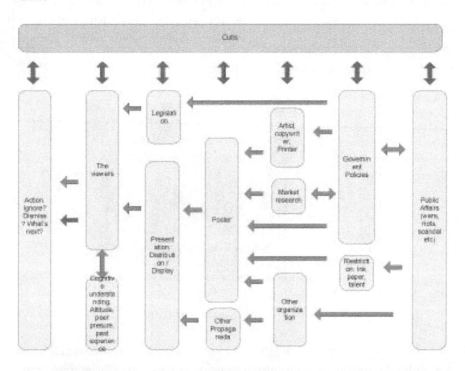

Ref-Code	From Component	To Component	Relationship	Description, Role of Cults
	Public Affairs	Public Affairs	NA	'We are everywhere public program' 'Integration through Enterprise Level Risk Management' Program

	Cults	Public affairs	Cults-> Public Affairs	Social Marketing Design and Realization: 'We are everywhere public' program 'Integration through Enterprise Level Risk Management' program
	Cults	Viewers	Cults-> Viewers	Assert the messages that 'Cults are everywhere', 'Cults manage your risks.' Bring them misfortune if necessary.
	Cults	Posters, Distribution Display	Cults-> Posters	Sponsor posters about what to display, what not to display
	Cults	Legislation	Cults-> Legislation	Manipulate legislator about what to pass, what not to pass.
	Cults	Organizations	Cults-> organizations	Work with organizations. Provide 'social support'. Fund or get funded to and from organizations. Make sure they accept the risk management package, otherwise bring them misfortune.
	Cults	Propaganda	Cults-> Propaganda	Use cult community mass media, publication and other information distribution channels to convey 'cults are everywhere, 'cults manage your risks.'.
	Cults	Government	Cults-> Government	Align goals with government. Get government support using bribery, donations, lobbying and threats. Bring government terrorism, if necessary.

	Government	Posters	Government-> Posters	Critical information needs to be distributed accurately, regardless it would create conflicts with cults.
	Government	Legislation	Government-> Legislation	Ensure legislation is run properly. Decision makers should legislate, based on public interests.
	Government	Organizations	Government-> Organizations	Government should enforce laws and restrictions to make sure organizations would not bring negative impact on public safety, healthcare, and welfare.
	Government	Propaganda	Government-> Propaganda	Government diverts the sense that, 'cults are everywhere', 'cults manage your risks.'
	Organization	Propaganda	Organization-> Propaganda	Help or not help cults to spread the messages, depending on corporate interests, and deal between cults and organizations.
	Poster / Propaganda	Distribution Display—Viewer	Poster / Propaganda-> Distribution-> Viewer	Viewers make critical decisions, based on what they see from the channels. They may join cult if they think this is the only way out else they get threatened.
	Viewer	Next Actions	Viewer-> Next Action	Viewers may or may not join cults based on rational and/or emotional decisions & considerations.

Interpersonal Perspectives Model (Model of Understanding and Misunderstanding)

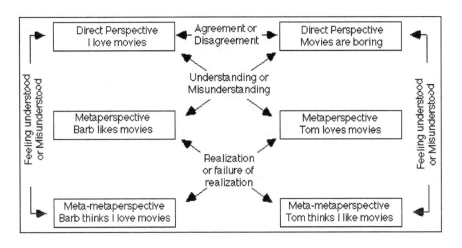

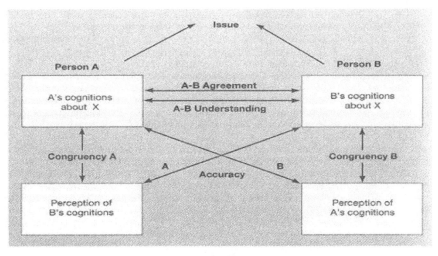

Fig 8-4. McLeod and Steven Interpersonal Perspectives Model
(Tomlison, 2000b).

The Conflict Model

The graph below uses 'level of violence' to define the stages of conflict. The nature of violence in conflict situations can be in many forms. However, bloodshed may not take place until conflict reaches a fairly mature stage.

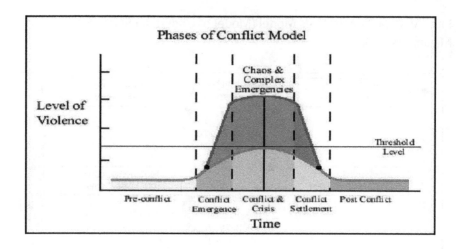

Fig 8-5 The Conflict Model—Crisis Lifecycle (Corrigan and Mortensen, 2004)

Caplan's Crisis Model

If Crisis slides towards a low point, coping strategies fail. Here people may seek relief from their helplessness by inappropriate means. Good support networks (helping forces from cults) enhance window of opportunity.

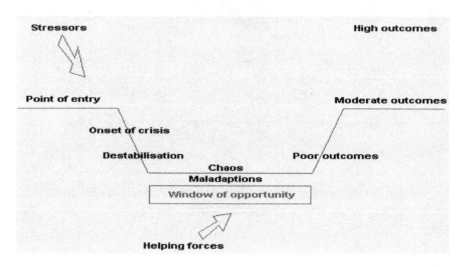

Fig 8-6. Caplan's Crisis Model (Corrigan and Mortensen, 2004b)

Social Marketing and Programming Models

Cult owners use three public media channels as marketing tools (Social Marketing). They want the news events from TV news channels to get synchronized with their live drama channel events.

All the actors are situated in a controlled, cultured, neutral platform, harassment-centric incumbents. These incumbents are managed by cults. Viewers just watch the channels without involvement.

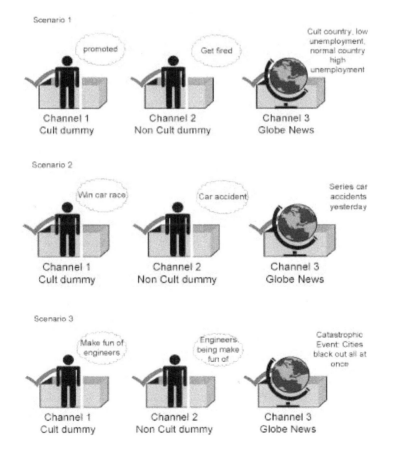

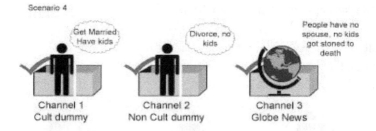

In general

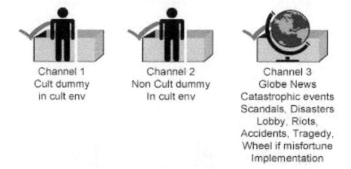

Blackout Example

Cults want to integrate themselves with electricity plant (Public utility).

As a live show, cults implement a catastrophic event in the power plant. Plant overloading happens, causing cascading failure with all electricity plants. The whole city gets a blackout. It takes few days to recover. People are scared without electricity and couple of people die because of this incident.

After the incident, the legislator and senators blame about lack of risk management causing the plant outage. They also blame the disaster recovery response for being slow. They are pushing government with new measures and policies to make sure the plant has enterprise-wide proper risk management programs and policies.

The cult professional risk management team approaches plant decision makers. Decision makers understand if they do not accept the service provided by the cult there is likely to be a revolution within the enterprise, and the same disaster is also likely to happen again.

They sign contracts and let cult members get in, and check current situation, suggest and execute improvement plan. No more disasters again. However, now people from the cults are working all over the plant. Hence, integration is successful.

Riot Example

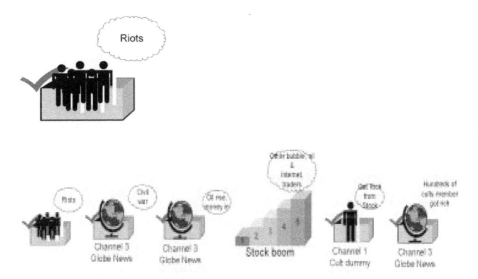

Initially people from the region are not happy. Cults initiate riots with the people of the region using Internet media such as Facebook groups. The effect of the riots is massive and critical such that the prime minister of the country gets overthrown, and the military starts getting involved. Military from other countries gets involved to support the riots. Civil war happens. The oil prices go up. In the Stock market, the value of energy stocks and Internet stocks start booming again. Cult members become millionaires since they know ahead itself that Internet bubble would come again, without knowing the reason why. They have already bought a lot of Internet stock at very low prices. Now they all make a fortune.

This can be known as 'ultimate' social integration, something that would give cult owners and leaders a high.

On the other hand the public asks themselves why there are so many mysterious coincidences? The events are so scattered and distributed, although the underlying message is united. This leads them to think that probably the magical hand behind these events is not human. Thus, joining the cult and worshipping perhaps are the only ways out.

9 DEPROGRAMMING

I am not a deprogrammer, but I may be perhaps responsible if anyone feels anxious after reading the previous chapters. This section will try to deprogram what you have been programmed for, in the previous chapters. I do hope readers find reading this book not only informative, but also therapeutic.

Deprogramming begins . . . .

The enterprise architecture views of cults are not real. All the models are not real. They are just imagination.

No one stalks me. No one has ever stalked me. There is no point organizations spend time resources to stalk me.

Cults are not real, there are nothing like cults in the real world. It is just a concept to justify people who feel who have been harassed by organizations.

No one harasses you. No one talks about you. You are the only one who can make yourself feel comfortable. Why would people spend so much effort to go after you and say something to make you uncomfortable? Why do you have to keep making yourself feel uncomfortable?

There are no cults in your community. Everyone wants to get themselves more involved in the community. They are not cults. It is just community involvement.

Do not think people are going to hurt you if you are not one of them. You are just paranoid. Why don't you see a doctor?

It is a public area. Everyone has the right to walk around here and talk. Why do you have to insist that they are stalking and harassing you?

There are no cults in the world. They are not cults. They are just friends in your neighborhood.

Even if you thought they were cults, it is fine now if you can forget about it.

Enjoy your life.

The enterprise architecture views of cults are not real. All the models are not real. They are just imagination.

No one stalks me. No one has ever stalked me. There is no point organizations spend time resources to stalk me.

Cults are not real, there are nothing like cults in the real world. It is just a concept to justify people who feel who have been harassed by organizations.

No one harasses you. No one talks about you. You are the only one who can make yourself feel comfortable. Why would people spend so much effort to go after you and say something to make you uncomfortable? Why do you have to keep making yourself feel uncomfortable?

There are no cults in your community. Everyone wants to get themselves more involved in the community. They are not cults. It is just community involvement.

Do not think people are going to hurt you if you are not one of them. You are just paranoid. Why don't you see a doctor?

It is a public area. Everyone has the right to walk around here and talk. Why do you have to insist that they are stalking and harassing you?

There are no cults in the world. They are not cults. They are just friends in your neighborhood.

Even if you thought they were cults, it is fine now if you can forget about it.

Enjoy your life.

The enterprise architecture views of cults are not real. All the models are not real. They are just imagination.

No one stalks me. No one has ever stalked me. There is no point organizations spend time resources to stalk me.

Cults are not real, there are nothing like cults in the real world. It is just a concept to justify people who feel who have been harassed by organizations.

No one harasses you. No one talks about you. You are the only one who can make yourself feel comfortable. Why would people spend so much effort to go after you and say something to make you uncomfortable? Why do you have to keep making yourself feel uncomfortable?

There are no cults in your community. Everyone wants to get themselves more involved in the community. They are not cults. It is just community involvement.

Do not think people are going to hurt you if you are not one of them. You are just paranoid. Why don't you see a doctor?

It is a public area. Everyone has the right to walk around here and talk. Why do you have to insist that they are stalking and harassing you?

There are no cults in the world. They are not cults. They are just friends in your neighborhood.

Even if you thought they were cults, it is fine now if you can forget about it.

Enjoy your life.

The enterprise architecture views of cults are not real. All the models are not real. They are just imagination.

No one stalks me. No one has ever stalked me. There is no point organizations spend time resources to stalk me.

Cults are not real, there are nothing like cults in the real world. It is just a concept to justify people who feel who have been harassed by organizations.

No one harasses you. No one talks about you. You are the only one who can make yourself feel comfortable. Why would people spend so much effort to go after you and say something to make you uncomfortable? Why do you have to keep making yourself feel uncomfortable?

There are no cults in your community. Everyone wants to get themselves more involved in the community. They are not cults. It is just community involvement.

Do not think people are going to hurt you if you are not one of them. You are just paranoid. Why don't you see a doctor?

It is a public area. Everyone has the right to walk around here and talk. Why do you have to insist that they are stalking and harassing you?

There are no cults in the world. They are not cults. They are just friends in your neighborhood.

Even if you thought they were cults, it is fine now if you can forget about it.

Enjoy your life.

Deprogramming ends . . .

APPENDIX A—REFERENCE

Websites

Dr. Tom O'Connor. (2011). Master Syllabi of required courses for the
BS degree in Criminal Justice/Homeland Security http://www.drtomoconnor.
com

Wikipedia: The free encyclopedia. (2011, July 15). FL: Wikimedia Foundation,
Inc. Retrieved July 15, 2011, from http://www.wikipedia.org

Books and Other Publications

Bennett, W. & Hess, K. (2007). Criminal investigation, 8e. Belmont, CA

Bromley, D. & Melton, J. (Eds.). (2002). Cults, Religion, and Violence. NY:
Cambridge Univ. Press.

Egger, S. (2002). The Killers Among Us. Upper Saddle River, NJ: Prentice Hall

Geberth, V. (2006). Practical Homicide Investigation. Boca Raton: CRC Press.

Hayes, S.C., Barnes-Holmes, D., & Roche, B. (Eds.) (2001). Relational Frame
Theory: A Post-Skinnerian Account of Human Language and Cognition. New
York: Plenum Publishers

Anthony Judge. (Image Maker). (2009). Indicative clustering of domains
implying various degrees of identification through geometric forms [Image],
Retrieved July 15, 2011, from: http://www.laetusinpraesens.org/musings/
idengeom.php

O'Connor, T. (2010). "Stalking" MegaLinks in Criminal Justice. Retrieved
from http://www.drtomoconnor.com/4050/4050lect06a.htm accessed on July
15, 2011.

O'Connor, T. (2010 Aug 23). "Becoming a Profiler" MegaLinks in Criminal
Justice. Retrieved from http://www.drtomoconnor.com/4050/4050lect01a.htm
accessed on July 15, 2011.

O'Connor, T. (2010 Aug 23 b). "How to Write A Profile Report" MegaLinks in Criminal Justice. Retrieved from http://www.drtomoconnor. com/4050/4050lect01b.htm accessed on July 15, 2011.

O'Connor, T. (2010 Aug 23 c). "Applied Criminology" MegaLinks in Criminal Justice. Retrieved from http://www.drtomoconnor.com/4050/4050lect02a.htm accessed on July 15, 2011

O'Connor, T. (2011). "Cult Crimes," MegaLinks in Criminal Justice. Retrieved from http://www.drtomoconnor.com/4050/4050lect06.htm accessed on July 15, 2011.

O'Connor, T. (2011 Mar 09). "Computer Hacker Typologies" MegaLinks in Criminal Justice. Retrieved from http://www.drtomoconnor. com/3400/3400lect06a.htm accessed on July 15, 2011

Rossmo, K. (2000). Geographic Profiling. Boca Raton: CRC Press.

Shawn Smith (2007). What is Relational Frame Theory, Retrieved July 15, 2011, from http://ironshrink.com/2007/12/what-is-relational-frame-theory-part-one/

Turvey, B. (1999). Criminal Profiling. San Diego: Academic Press.

Turvey, B. (2002). Criminal Profiling, 2e. San Diego: Academic Press.

Wood, R. & Wood, N. (2002). "Stalking the stalker." FBI Law Enforcement Bulletin 7(12)

Definitions

1984. (2011.July 15.). In Wikipedia. Retrieved July 15, 2011, from http:// en.wikipedia.org/wiki/Nineteen_Eighty-Four

1Q84. (2011.July 15.). In Wikipedia. Retrieved July 15, 2011, from http:// en.wikipedia.org/wiki/1Q84

Enterprise architecture. (2011.July 15.). In Wikipedia. Retrieved July 15, 2011, from http://en.wikipedia.org/wiki/Enterprise_architecture

Harassment. (2011.July 12.). In Wikipedia. Retrieved July 15, 2011, from http://en.wikipedia.org/wiki/Harassment

Trespass. (2011.June 26.). In Wikipedia. Retrieved July 15, 2011, from http:// en.wikipedia.org/wiki/Trespass

Harassment. (2011.July 15.). In definition-of.net. Retrieved July 15, 2011, from http://www.definition-of.net/harassment

Sovereign. (2011.July 15.). In The free dictionary by Farlex,. Retrieved July 15, 2011, from http://legal-dictionary.thefreedictionary.com/Sovereign+power

Electronic Images

Matt Armstrong (Image Maker). (2007). Smart Power Equalizer [Images], Retrieved July 15, 2011, from http://mountainrunner.us/2007/02/smart_power_equalizer_finding.html

Corrigan and Mortensen (Image Maker). (2004). The Conflict Model—Crisis Life Cycle [Images], Retrieved July 15, 2011 from http://users.marshall.edu/~corrigan/default.htm

Corrigan and Mortensen (Image Maker). (2004b). Caplan's Crisis Model [Images], Retrieved July 15, 2011 from http://users.marshall.edu/~corrigan/default.htm

Nicolas Cuperlier, Mathias Quoy and Philippe Gaussier (Image Maker). (2007). Interaction between the cognitive map and the transitions. [Images], Retrieved July 15, 2011, from http://www.frontiersin.org/neurorobotics/10.3389/neuro.12.003.2007/full

Denis Fleming (Image Maker). (Date). The NLP Model [Images], Retrieved July 15, 2011, from http://www.denisfleming.com/eft-nlp.html

Anthony Judge. (Image Maker). (2009). Indicative clustering of domains implying various degrees of identification through geometric forms [Image], Retrieved July 15, 2011, from: http://www.laetusinpraesens.org/musings/idengeom.php

Happe (Image Maker). (2009). Community Maturity Model [Images], Retrieved July 15, 2011 from http://community-roundtable.com/2009/06/the-community-maturity-model/

Kinyofu Mteremeshi-Mlimwengu (Image Maker). (2011). Emotion Wheel of regular emotion states [Images], Retrieved July 15, 2011, from http://selfreflection.empoweringwomenslives.com/?p=1006

Klaus von Lampe (Image Maker). (2003). Causal Model [Images], Retrieved July 15, 2011, from http://www.organized-crime.de/modelsofoc.htm

Klaus von Lampe (Image Maker). (2003b). Analytic Model [Images], Retrieved July 15, 2011, from http://www.organized-crime.de/modelsofoc.htm

Shawn Smith. (Image Maker). (2007). The standard, overly complicated communication model [Images], Retrieved July 15, 2011, from http://ironshrink.com/2007/12/what-is-relational-frame-theory-part-one/

Shawn Smith. (Image Maker). (2007b). Training the dog [Images], Retrieved July 15, 2011, from http://ironshrink.com/2007/12/what-is-relational-frame-theory-part-one/

Shawn Smith. (Image Maker). (2007c). Training the dog [Images], Retrieved July 15, 2011, from http://ironshrink.com/2007/12/what-is-relational-frame-theory-part-one/

Shawn Smith. (Image Maker). (2007c). Training the baby [Images], Retrieved July 15, 2011, from http://ironshrink.com/2007/12/what-is-relational-frame-theory-part-one/

Tomlison (Image Maker). (2000). Lievrouw and Finn's Communication Systems [Images], Retrieved July 15, 2011, from http://faculty.evansville.edu/dt4/301/primer301.html

Tomlison (Image Maker). (2000b). McLeod and Steven Interpersonal Perspectives Model [Images], Retrieved July 15, 2011, from http://faculty.evansville.edu/dt4/301/primer301.html

Verma, Arvind and S. K. Lodha (Image Maker). (2002). Spatial and Temporal Model [Images], Retrieved July 15, 2011, from http://wcr.sonoma.edu/v3n2/verma.html

Offline PC Electronic Games

TECMO KOEI CO. LTD. (Screen Shots). (2005). SANGO 1-13 [PC game Screen shots]. Tokyo

SQUARE ENIX (Screen Shots). (2008). Final Fantasy [PC game Screen shots], Tokyo

UserJoy Technology. (2006). Angel Love [PC game Screen shots], Tapei

APPENDIX B—ZACHMAN ENTERPRISE ARCHITECTURE FRAMEWORK

The Zachman Framework is an Enterprise Architecture framework for enterprise architecture, which provides a formal and highly structured way of viewing and defining an enterprise. It consists of a two dimensional classification matrix based on the intersection of six communication questions (What, Where, When, Why, Who and How) with six rows according to reification transformations.

	Why	How	What	Who	Where	When
Contextual	Goal List	Process List	Material List	Organizational Unit & Role List	Geographical Locations List	Event List
Conceptual	Goal Relationship	Process Model	Entity Relationship Model	Organizational Unit & Role Rel. Model	Locations Model	Event Model
Logical	Rules Diagram	Process Diagram	Data Model Diagram	Role relationship Diagram	Locations Diagram	Event Diagram
Physical	Rules Specification	Process Function Specification	Data Entity Specification	Role Specification	Location Specification	Event Specification
Detailed	Rules Details	Process Details	Data Details	Role Details	Location details	Event Details

The Zachman "Framework" is a taxonomy for organizing architectural artifacts (in other words, design documents, specifications, and models) that takes into account both whom the artifact targets (for example, business owner and builder) and what particular issue (for example, data and functionality) is being addressed. (Wikipedia 2011)